The Romance

of the

Cheuelere Assigne.

re-edited by

Henry H. Gibbs

EARLY ENGLISH TEXT SOCIETY

Extra Series, 6

1868

Extra Series, vi.

The Romance

of the

Cheuelere Assigne.

RE-EDITED FROM

THE UNIQUE MANUSCRIPT IN THE BRITISH MUSEUM,

WITH A PREFACE, NOTES, AND GLOSSARIAL INDEX,

BY

HENRY H. GIBBS, ESQ., M.A.

OF EXETER COLLEGE, OXFORD.

LONDON:
PUBLISHED FOR THE EARLY ENGLISH TEXT SOCIETY
By HUMPHREY MILFORD, OXFORD UNIVERSITY PRESS,
AMEN HOUSE, E.C.4.
1868 (reprinted 1898, 1932).

OXFORD

UNIVERSITY PRESS

Great Clarendon Street, Oxford OX2 6DP
United Kingdom

Oxford University Press is a department of the University of Oxford.
It furthers the University's objective of excellence in research, scholarship,
and education by publishing worldwide. Oxford is a registered trade mark of
Oxford University Press in the UK and in certain other countries

© The Early English Text Society 1868

The moral rights of the authors have been asserted

Database right Oxford University Press (maker)

First Edition published in paperback 1868

All rights reserved. No part of this publication may be reproduced,
stored in a retrieval system, or transmitted, in any form or by any means,
without the prior permission in writing of Oxford University Press,
or as expressly permitted by law, or under terms agreed with the appropriate
reprographics rights organization. Enquiries concerning reproduction
outside the scope of the above should be sent to the Rights Department,
Oxford University Press, at the address above

You must not circulate this book in any other form
and you must impose this same condition on any acquirer

Published in the United States of America by Oxford University Press
198 Madison Avenue, New York, NY 10016, United States of America

British Library Cataloguing in Publication Data
Data available

Library of Congress Cataloging in Publication Data
Data available

Extra Series, 6

ISBN 978-0-85-991876-3

PREFACE.

THIS short alliterative poem has already been edited by Mr Utterson, and presented by him in 1820 to the members of the Roxburghe Club ; but as the few copies then printed are very rare, and as the work is a curious specimen of unrimed alliterative poetry of a comparatively late date, it has been thought worth while that it should be edited again for the Extra Series of the Early English Text Society.

A mere reprint of the former edition would not have been desirable, both because there are several mistranscriptions, and because the glossary appended to that edition is excessively meagre, and in some cases erroneous : but so much advance has been made since the date of that publication in the knowledge of our ancient tongue, that however much this edition may leave to be desired, there will be no great difficulty in correcting the errors of the former one.

Wherever the new transcript differed from the Roxburghe edition, I have with especial care compared it with the manuscript, so as to satisfy myself of the correctness of the new reading.

The poem consists of 370 lines ; and is contained, with other pieces, in Caligula A. 2 of the Cotton MSS. in the British Museum. It professes to be taken from some other book (in the 7th line and elsewhere the author uses the expression, ' as þe book tellethe '), and appears to be an epitome of the first 1083 lines of the French poem, or rather 'lay' (in the sense in which Scott uses the word), which forms part of the volume marked 15 E. vj in the Royal Collection in the same library.

This French Manuscript contains many beautiful illuminations of excellent workmanship, two of which adorn the head of the first page (fo. 320) of the ' Chevalier au Signe.' The left-hand picture represents Queen Bietrix (as she is there called) sitting up in bed and looking very unhappy, while ' Matebrune' is carrying away a cot (nearly as big as the Queen's bed) with the seven children in it, clad four in green and three in purple, placed alternately. The right-hand picture represents the Knight ' Helyas,' armed, and in his ship alone ; the

Swan, 'ducally gorged, Or,' as a herald would say, sailing proudly before him. This picture is very like one of the compartments of the Ivory Casket, to which I shall presently refer.

Meanwhile, as this French chanson—so its author frequently calls it [1]—appears to be the original from whence our English author drew his poem, I will give an outline of the longer history told in its 6000 lines, comparing it from time to time with the very entertaining English Prose Romance, printed by Copland early in the 16th century, and edited in 1858 by Mr Thoms.

THE STORY OF THE KNIGHT OF THE SWAN.

Briefly told it is as follows:

Beatrix, Queen of King Oryens of Lilefort, after some years of childlessness, conceived seven children at one burden (as a punishment for disbelieving the possibility of twins being begotten by one man); and when she is brought to bed, in her husband's absence, his mother substitutes seven puppies for the seven children, whom she consigns to Marques, or Marcon, a serf of hers, with orders for their murder: when the King returns she shows him the whelps as the Queen's offspring, and demands her death; but the King only allows her to be imprisoned.

The children (who were miraculously born with silver chains about their necks) are of course not slain, but fed by a hind in the forest, and tended by a hermit in his cell.

They are unfortunately seen by the Forester Mauquarre, or Malquarrez, who tells the Queen; and by her desire he goes back to kill them and take away their chains. One, however, who is the hero of the tale, has gone out with the hermit to get food for the others; so that the forester finds only six of the children, and deprives them of their chains, upon which they are transformed into swans.

---

[1] The poem begins '*Escoutez seigneurs pour Dieu lespitable
  Que Ihus vous garisse de lamain au D*yable;'
and every now and then the minstrel addresses his hearers to call their attention to his song. Thus when Elyas first comes to Nimaye, the next sentence begins '*Seigneurs oez chancon qui moult fait aloer*.' After the battle with the friends of the prevost, comes, '*Seigneurs or escoutez chancon de grant baronaige;*' and again, '*Seigneurs or escoutez bonne chancon;*' and '*Seigneurs oez chancon de bonne enluminee;*' and '*Seigneurs oyez chancon qui est vray.*'

The old Queen questions Marcon, and revenges herself on him by putting out his eyes.

When the Queen has been 11 years in prison, Matebrune prevails on the King to condemn her to be burnt; and the day is fixed accordingly, and she is led to the stake.

Meanwhile an angel appears to the hermit and orders that the child should go to the city, be christened Helyas, and fight for his mother. He does so, meets the procession, accosts the King, obtains his consent to the battle, borrows from him horse and armour, slays Mauquarre, who is the champion on behalf of the accuser, and frees his mother.

Matebrune flees to a castle; Helyas prays to God, who restores Marques's sight. He tells his story to his newly-found father and mother, and all the court go to the water where the swans are swimming, and, their chains being restored to them, they resume their human form; all but one, who remains a swan.

Up to this time, as will be seen, the English poem faithfully accompanies the French one, excepting that as the poet means to make an end here, he summarily burns Matabryne, and says that the 6th brother continued *always* a swan for lack of his chain.

Moreover he makes no mention of the miracle of healing done on Marcus.

The French story proceeds with the abdication of King Oriant (on the plea that he has now lived a long time—*plus que c. ans*—) in favour of Helyas; with the siege of Matebrune's castle, the death of her champion Hendrys by the hand of Helyas; her capture, confession, and burning; whereafter

'*Lame emporterent dyables ; ce fut la destinee.*'

The angel then appears to King Helyas and bids him leave his father and mother, and seek adventures under the guidance of his brother the swan, who waits for him with '*ung batel.*'

He abdicates, and leaves the kingdom to Orions, and divers governments to his other brothers.

From this differs the English Prose Romance of the Knight of the Swan, which makes no mention of King Oryens' great age, but makes

King Helyas surrender the kingdom again into his hands. Neither does he mention Helyas's departure at the bidding of the angel; but makes the swan-brother summon him by 'mervaylous cries,' to come into the boat which he has brought, and which he guides, without further adventure, to the city of Nimaye.

But in the French story he arrives soon at a city of Saracens, who assault him and his swan;—but he is rescued by 30 galleys under the guidance of Saint George (*qui fut bon chevalier*); and the four winds also helped, raising a storm and drowning the Saracens.

It then tells how Elyas went on alone in his boat, with the swan, till they came to a castle, called Sauvage, whose master was Agolant, brother of Matebrune; how their provisions being exhausted, they sought help at the castle; how Agolant received him well, but, after hearing his story, seizes, imprisons, and promises to burn him eight days thereafter.

But a page escapes and goes to Lilefort to King Orions, who goes with a great force to succour his brother. The men arrive when Helyas is already bound at the stake, and Agolant and all his men have to go out to repel them;—a friendly hand releases Helyas, who joins his brother's men, and slays Agolant.

Oryons goes back to Lilefort, and Helyas, summoning his brother the swan, pursues his way to Nimaye.

There, in a tournament, he slays an Earl [of Francbourck, says Copland], who, in a false plea before the Emperor Otho, is trying to deprive [Clarysse] Duchess Dabullon [of Bouillon] of her lands; and wins for himself the lands of Ardennes [of Dardaigne, in Copland] belonging to the Earl; and also gets to wife Beatrice, the fair daughter and heiress of the Duchess, by whom he has a daughter Idein or Ydain, who in time becomes the mother of Godfrey of Bouillon.

He leaves Nimaye and goes to his duchy of Bouillon, conquering in the way *Asselm le prevost* and many partisans of the deceased Earl, who had laid an ambush for him.

Many perilous adventures then befell him in Bouillon, which are recounted at considerable length; and afterwards the story tells how that, his wife having disobeyed his commandment which he laid upon her, not to inquire concerning his kith and kin, he departs from her, and rides away to Nimaye, to take leave of the Emperor, and bespeak his protection for his wife, daughter, and lands.

Thence, amidst great lamentation of the Emperor and all his barons, he departs in his boat with his brother the swan, and no more is known of him.

Oncq ne sceurent quelle part y fu tournes.

Then it passes on to tell of Godfrey Earl of Bouillon, his birth and deeds. How with the leave of the Emperor, Eustace Earl of '*Boulogne sur mer salee*' went a courting to Ydain '*a la fresce coulour*' (daughter of Helyas), then aged 13 years; how he married her; and how in the three years following she had three fair sons, Godfrey, Baldwin, and Eustace; and how that the eldest after many noble deeds went to Palestine, and took the Holy City. The poem ends with the assault and capture of Jerusalem and the crowning of Godfrey as its King.

The English Prose Romance takes up the story of Helyas where the French Poem leaves him, and tells how he arrived at Lilefort and is welcomed by his father and mother after his viij years' absence.

The Queen, it tells us, had a dream, in which she dreams that if they get the two cups which had been made of the 6th son's chain, and lay them on two altars, and set the swan on a bed betwixt the altars, and cause two masses to be said by devout priests who shall consecrate in the two chalices, the swan shall return to his own form: and 'Ryght so,' says Copland, 'as the priests consacred the body of our Lorde at the masse, the swanne retourned into his propre fourme and was a man,' and he was baptized, and named Emery.

'The whiche sith was a noble knight.'

'And thus,' he says, 'the noble king Oriant and the good queene Beatrice finabli recovered all their children by the grace of God, wherfore fro than forthon they lived holyly and devoutly in our Lorde.'

Now King Oriant had 'made a Religion' at the hermitage where his son Helyas had been brought up; and thither, after recounting his adventures, the good Knight of the Swan betook himself, with a simple staff in his hand, and made himself a 'Religious.'

And close to the convent he caused to be built a castle like to that of Bouillon, and he called it Bouillon, and the forest that was about it he called Dardayne, after the land that he had won from the Earl.

The English story here goes on to tell of the marriage of Eustace Earl of Boulogne and Ydain daughter of Helyas, and of the birth of her sons Godfrey, Baldwin, and Eustace ; and how that her mother, the Duchess of Bouillon, lamenting for the loss of her husband Helyas, sent messengers all over the world to find him ; and how that Ponce, one of these messengers, went to Jerusalem, and meeting there the Abbot Girarde of Saincteron, which is nigh to Bouillon, they determined as fellow-countrymen to return together. How they lose their way, and come to the castle of Bouillon *le restaure*, and are struck by the likeness to their own Bouillon ; how they inquire of the Curate, and hear who it was who built the castle and named the forest.

And how that they make themselves known to Emery and Helyas, and also to the King and Queen, who had come to live at the castle, and how they returned to their country, bearing a token from Helyas to his wife.

Then it tells how the Duchess and the Countess Ydain, whose sons were by this time adolescent, set forth to see their husband and father Helyas, and how they found him lying sick unto death, and how shortly thereafter 'he desceased in our lorde Jesu Chryst.'

How the ladies returned to Bouillon, and how the three noble brethren prepared themselves by a knightly education for the day when it should please God to give the kingdom of Jerusalem into the hands of Godfrey of Bouillon, the eldest born. 'And thus,' says Copland, 'endeth the life and myraculous hystory of the most noble and illustryous Helyas knight of the swanne, with the birth of the excellent knyght Godfrey of Boulyon, one of the nyne worthiest, and the last of the three crysten.'

The English romance, printed by Copland, is in some parts much fuller even than the French poem, going more into detail as to the wooing of King Oryens, and the cause of the enmity of Matabryne ; but here and there the French 'chanson' has details which Copland's book does not give ; such as the troublous adventures of

Helyas in his journey between Lilefort and Nimaye, and the acts and prowess of Godfrey, and his conquest of his kingdom; but as to the legendary hero of the story, the Knight of the Swan, the tale of his deeds until his retirement from the world is mainly the same, in the English prose and in the French verse.

THE CASKET.

This curious work, of which I have before made mention, is an ancient ivory one, of 14th-century workmanship, now belonging to Mr William Gibbs of Tyntesfield, co. Somerset, and formerly to his wife's family, the Crawley-Boeveys, Baronets, of Flaxley Abbey, co. Gloucester. It is 8 inches long, $5\frac{3}{4}$ deep, and $5\frac{1}{4}$ inches high; and in its thirty-six compartments it gives the history of the Knight of the Swan; going no further than our poem, except that it depicts the capture of Matabryne's castle and the leave-taking and departure of Helyas. It is this last compartment that so nearly resembles the illumination at the head of the French poem.

I now proceed to describe the carvings in the several compartments, which are all of them remarkable for their accurate detail of arms and costume, and some groups, especially in Nos. 23 and 24, very spirited in their execution.

The top of the casket.

1. The King, Queen, and Matabryne on the wall. Mother and Twins below.
2. The King and the Queen in bed.
3. The King discovers that the Queen is with child.
4. The Queen asleep in bed: Matabryne carries off the children.
5. Matabryne delivers the children to Marcus.
6. Matabryne drowns the bitch in a well.
7. Matabryne presents the whelps to the King, who wrings his hands.
8. Marcus exposes the children in the forest.
9. Malkedras (?) thrusts the Queen into prison.
10. The hermit finds the children.
11. A hind suckles them; and Malkedras finds them.
12. Malkedras tells Matabryne.

The front of the casket.

13. Malkedras takes the chains from the children's necks.
14. They fly away as swans.
15. Matabryne praises and caresses Malkedras.
16. Matabryne taunts the King, and gets leave to burn the Queen.
17. A soldier is leading the Queen to execution: she has fallen on her knees and is praying. See l. 90, note.
18. The King is on his throne as if to see the burning. Matabryne and a man in armour behind him, counselling him.
19. The angel appears to the hermit and the child.
20. The hermit and the child set forth on their way.

The left side of the casket.

21. The King on his throne; the Queen presents the child as her champion, and Matabryne Malkedras as hers.
22. Combat between Helyas and Malkedras.
23. Helyas having slain Malkedras, bears away his head.
24. Flight of Matabryne.

The back of the casket.

25. Helyas presents the head of Malkedras to the King.
26. Reconciliation of King Oryens and Queen Beatrice.
27. The King and Queen embrace Helyas.
28. King Helyas with a kneeling figure before him. He seems to be giving something into his hand; and perhaps it is a commission to a captain 'to prepaire a lytle hoste,' as Copland has it.
29. His army march against Matabryne.
30. They prepare to assault
31. The castle and its defenders.
32. Capture of Matabryne.

The right side of the casket.

33. Helyas recounts his adventures to his father and mother.
34. The burning of Matabryne.

35. The King and the Queen gazing

36. At Helyas departing in his ship alone, led by his brother the swan.

The letter from Mr Dallaway, and extract of a letter from Mr Vay in the note below, give the opinion of those antiquaries on the late and artistic value of this casket.[1]

---

[1] 'Mr Dallaway's respectful compliments to Sir Thomas Crawley, with the cabinet he has so long detained. He should have returned it with more satisfaction had he been able to discover the whole of the history represented, which is too complicated for him to unravel.

'Upon the upper compartment is evidently shown the well-known Legend of Isenbard, Earl of Altorf, and Irmentruda his wife, with her supernatural progeny.

'The two sons, who were preserved, were called Guelfo and Ghibelino, and their descendants were leaders of the factions by which the Italian States were distracted in the 12th century.

'He is of opinion that the remainder of their legendary story is described round the sides of the cabinet, and is not without hopes that, when he can meet with a very scarce collection of German novels, entitled "Camerarii Horæ Subcesivæ," it will furnish him with the whole of the detail.

'The armour and weapons of some of the figures are decidedly those of the 4th century, when elaborate carving was in very general use, and many Greek artists were encouraged; which circumstance seems to establish the date of the specimen.

'The enclosed drawing Mr D. begs that Sir Thomas will accept, with many thanks, for the permission he has obtained to have it etched. He will take care that justice be done to it, and hopes that Sir T. will find room in his portfolio for some of the proof impressions.

'Jan. 5, 1793.

'Sir Thomas Crawley.'

'*Wonham Manor,*
'*Reigate, Nov.* 29, '60.

'Dear Sir Martin,

'Your kindness in permitting me to bring home your curious ivory casket has, as I anticipated, enabled me to ascertain the whole of the subjects represented upon it. After much fruitless research, and showing the casket to several learned friends, I have at length got the right clue, and all difficulty ceases. The subjects are all from one romance, known as the " Knight of the Swan," and not found in any of the abstracts of middle-age romances, by Ellis, Dunlop, or the Italian writer Ferrario. It has, however, been published, but the volumes containing it are of very great rarity.

'I hope to send you an account of the romance, detailing the subjects as they occur on the casket. . . . .

. . . . I should almost suggest only to repair the broken portions of the metal bands as they exist, not to renew those which have been

ORIGIN OF THE ROMANCE.

Little or nothing can be added, on this head, to what Mr Thoms has collected in his preface to the Knight of the Swan; and what I here write is chiefly drawn from that source.

Mr Utterson quotes Mr F. Cohen (Sir Francis Palgrave) for the opinion that the earliest form in which the story exists is in the Chronicle of Tongres, written by the Maitre de Guise, and incorporated in great part into the Mer des Hystoires. There is also, he says, an Icelandic Saga of Helis, the Knight of the Swan, in which he is called a son of Julius Cæsar; and a similar legend is introduced into the German romance of *Lohengrin*, of which an edition was printed at Heidelberg as late as 1813. The story is still popular in Flanders, where a Chap-book, entitled De Ridder Met de Zwaen, was of frequent occurrence early in this century.

The immediate parent of the English prose romances on the subject appears to be the French folio printed in 1504, and entitled LA GENEALOGIE AVECQUES LES GESTES ET NOBLES FAITZ DARMES DU TRES PREUX ET RENOMME PRINCE GODEFFROY DE BOULION ET DE SES CHEUALEREUX FRERES BAUDOUIN ET EUSTACE, YSSUS & DESCENDUS DE LA TRES NOBLE & ILLUSTRE LIGNEE DU VERTUEUX CHEVALIER AU CYNE. AVECQUES AUSSI PLUSIEURS AUTRES CRONIQUES HYSTOIRES MIRACULEUSES; TANT DU BON ROY SAINCT LOYS COMME DE PLUSIEURS AULTRES PUISSANS & VERTUEUX CHEVALIERS.

It was the first thirty-eight chapters of this work that were published in an English form by Robert Copland (which is the version edited by Mr Thoms); and Ames speaks of a translation published by Wynkyn de Worde, in 1512; but it is not now known to exist.

lost. . . . . It is to be considered that these metal bands are not original. The ivory dates from about 1380; the metal work about 1550.
. . . .
'Believe me, very sincerely yours,
'ALBERT WAY.'
'Sir Martin Crawley-Boevey.'

Mr Way says in another letter that photographs had been taken of the casket. These I have never seen, but a set has been prepared expressly for this edition.

The tradition that the great Godfrey of Bouillon was descended from the Knight of the Swan, has always been a favourite one, and one of the most interesting stories in Otmar's Volksagen is founded on it. Nicolas de Klerc, in order to set right the common opinion in Flanders,

> Om dat van Brabant die Hertoghen
> Voormaels, dicke syn beloghen
> Alse dat sy quamen metten Swane
>
> [Forasmuch as the Dukes of Brabant
> have been heretofore much belied
> as that they came with a Swan],

professes to tell the truth about it in his Brabandshe Yeesten, written in 1318; and Marlaent refers to the same belief in his Spiegel Historiael.

On the other hand (through Godfrey, no doubt,) Robert Copland claims it as an honour for his patron, Edward Duke of Buckingham, that from the Knight of the Swan 'linially is dyscended my sayde Lorde.'

As to the portentous birth, which is the basis of the story, similar tales have been not unfrequently told. Amongst others there is one in which the house of Guelph is said to take its name from a like incident.

'Irmentrudes, wife of Isenbard Earl of Altorfe, accused a woman of adultery for bringing forth three children at a birth; adding withal that she was worthy to be sown in a sack, and thrown into the sea; and urged it very earnestly. It chanced in the year following, that she herself conceived, and in the absence of her husband, was delivered of twelve male children at one birth (though very little). But she, fearing the imputation and scandal she had formerly laid on the poor woman, and the law of like for like, caused her most trusty woman to make choice of one to be tendered to the father, and to drown all the residue in a neighbouring river. It fell out that the Earl Isenbard returning home, met this woman, demanding whither she went with her pail? who answered, "to drown a few baggage whelps in the river." The Earl would see them; and notwithstanding the woman's resistance, did so, and discovering the children, pressed her to tell the matter, which she also did; and he caused them all to be secretly nursed ; and, grown great, were brought home unto him, which he placed in an open hall with the son whom his wife had brought up, and soon known to be brethren by their likelihood in every respect. The Countess confessed the whole matter (moved with the sting of conscience), and was forgiven. In remembrance whereof, the illustrious race of the Welfes (whelps) got that name, and ever since hath kept it.'

Westcote (whose words I transcribe, as his book is a privately printed one (1845) from his MS. c. 1600) quotes this story from one Camerarius (he says) of Nuremberg, as a companion to a story of the wife of a peasant of Chumleigh, co. Devon, who had seven children at a birth, and whose husband, for fear of having to maintain so many mouths, resolves to drown them, and declares to the Countess of Devon, who meets him while on his errand, that they are but whelps. She rescues them and provides for them.

In French history we have a story somewhat analogous, in the efforts of the monks to separate Robert Capet and his wife, by persuading him that she had given birth to a monster.

The after part of the story of our book is the old one told with many variations from the time of the Shepherd David until now, of extreme youth, with the aid of the grace of God, vanquishing in battle the evil-doer, though a man of war from his youth.

THE VERSIFICATION OF THE POEM.

Coming now to the versification of the poem : I have thought it useful to analyse it so as to ascertain how far the author has kept himself to the rules of alliterative verse, as collected by Mr Skeat in his Essay on the subject prefixed to the 3rd volume of the Percy Folio.

The author seems to have contented himself with preserving generally the proper swing of his metre, the accentuated syllables marking it, in most cases, fairly well: but it often halts, the soft or unaccentuated syllables being awkwardly and too prodigally used, and the rime-letters very frequently falling on those syllables.

In many couplets the alliteration is utterly irregular, and in 10 couplets[1] I can discover none at all.

[1] 21, 34, 106, 225, 232, 334-6, 343, 367.

In 22 others[1] he has satisfied himself with a feeble sprinkling of the same letter through the verse without any regard to the loud syllables; as

  60. *at a* chamber dore *a*s she forth sowȝte

sometimes also supplementing the weakness of one alliteration by adding a second in the same couplet; as

  241. that *s*tyked *s*tyffe in her Brestes · þat wolde þe qwene BRe*n*ne
  287. A *k*nyȝte *k*awȝte Hym by þe Honde · & ladde Hym of þe route.

The couplets in which there are but two rime-letters are very many; no less than 143[2] out of the whole number of 370; and there are eight couplets[3] with four rime-letters.

The other variations from the established rule are: (*a*.) The occurrence of the chief letter on the second instead of the first loud syllable of the second line, which is found 64 times,[4] and of these 64, 29 ([5]) occur in couplets with but two rime-letters.

(*b*.) The occurrence of two rime-letters in the second line of the couplet, and but one in the first, in 37 couplets.[6]

(*c*.) The absence of the chief letter in the second limb of the couplet occurs 20 times.[7]

(*d*.) The rime-letters occur very often indeed upon unaccentuated or 'soft' syllables; so often, as to lead one to think that the author must have deemed his task fully done, if only there was any alliteration at all. The number is 72,[8] besides three in the next class.

---

[1] 13-4, 32, 49, 52, 60, 81, 96, 113, 132, 145, 158, 165, 185, 199, 210-1, 218, 272, 281-2, 351.

[2] 5, 6, 8, 10-1, 16, 24, 30-1, 40-1, 45-6, 54, 58, 63, 65, 75-6, 80, 82, 88, 90, 95, 99, 101, 103-5, 108, 110, 114-5, 120-1, 127-9, 137, 139, 142, 146, 149-50, 154-5, 160-2, 166-7, 172, 174, 181, 184, 189, 191-2, 195-6, 200-1, 208, 222, 227-9, 231, 240-1, 244, 247, 250-3, 256, 258, 264-5, 268-9, 271, 273, 280, 285-6, 290, 292, 294, 296, 299, 300, 302-6, 309, 314-6, 320-1, 323, 325, 327-8, 338, 353-4, 368-70.

[3] 2, 35, 42, 91, 152, 183, 239, 360.

[4] 1, 4, 20, 25-6, 30, 42, 53, 69, 70, 112, 136, 156, 173, 179, 183, 202, 212, 217, 226, 236, 239, 248, 261, 295, 310, 313, 317, 319, 324, 329, 331, 334, 355, 359. ([5]) 22, 37-8, 48, 56, 64, 86, 123, 140, 144, 164, 177, 182, 187-8, 190, 194, 203, 205-6, 207, 214, 236, 238, 246, 254, 308, 312, 363.

[6] 1, 12, 17, 23, 51, 78-9, 83-4, 107, 119, 135, 138, 141, 151, 159, 169, 170, 175, 198, 209, 223, 233-5, 237, 243, 255, 291, 293, 326, 340-2, 350, 356-7.

[7] 19, 50, 59, 67, 125, 153, 157, 163, 215, 219, 257, 259, 277, 279, 289, 332, 346-7, 352, 364.

[8] 2, 7, 23, 25-6, 28, 31, 35, 39, 40, 50-1, 66, 70, 73, 77, 79, 82, 102-3, 108-9,

(e.) Where the chief letter occurs in the initial catch of the second couplet.[1]

There are also *ten* couplets[2] with separate alliterations in each line, and

Seven,[3] in which there are no rime-letters in the first line.

And the couplets that appear to conform strictly to the canon of alliteration which provides that there shall be three rime-letters in each couplet, viz. two (sub-letters) in the accentuated syllables of the first line or limb of it, and one (the chief letter) on the first accentuated syllable of the second line, are 48 in number;[4] such as

  92. Now Leve we þis Lady · in Langour & pyne
  147. They sToden alle sTylle · for sTere þey ne durste

But of these 48, the alliteration is not always perfect, *w* having to do duty with words beginning with Oo (l. 29); *D* being once used as a rime-letter to *T* (l. 27), and the *G* in gladness being once considered mute, so as to rime the word with 'lay in langour' (l. 57).

The former editor draws attention to the existence of some rime-endings in this poem, but they seem to me to be accidental rather than intentional.

Mr Skeat enumerates them in his essay, and I set them down here, excepting those in lines 260-1, where he has been misled by the former editor's mistaking the long second *r* in *marre*, and reading it *marye;* and in 28, 29, where the editor has mistaken *leue* for *lene;*

 12-13, *where* and *there*
 31-32, *were* and *there*
 158-159, *swyde* and *leyde*. This is not a rime at all.
 166-167, *faste* and *caste*
 198-199,}
 350-351,} *swannes* and *cheynes*. A very doubtful rime.

116, 118, 120, 126-8, 141, 143, 152, 156, 159, 161, 168-9, 175-6, 178, 180, 186, 191, 195, 202, 204, 209, 217, 220-1, 234-5, 250, 256, 261-2, 267, 270, 274, 278, 280, 283-4, 287-8, 292, 294, 337, 341, 343, 347-8, 357.

[1] 55, 75, 96.
[2] 44, 72, 85, 111, 216, 249, 266, 275, 330, 365.
[3] 117, 198, 245, 318, 345, 350, 362.
[4] 3, 9, 15, 18, 27, 29, 33, 36, 39, 43, 47, 57, 61-2, 71, 74, 87, 89, 91-4, 97-8, 100, 124, 131, 133-4, 147-8, 171, 193, 197, 213, 260, 263, 276, 297-8, 301, 307, 311, 322, 339, 349, 360-1, 366.

237-238, *were* and *mysfare;*
and I may add 359-60, *made* and *bledde.*

But among these there are but three rimes which are at all perfect; and it may be observed that in the 370 lines (from 200 to 570) of William of Palerne, which I have searched cursorily, there are as many:

As, 210, þat of horne ne of *hounde* · ne mizt he here *sowne*

236-7, *telle* and *wille*

337-8, *speche* and *riche*

404, as euene as ani *wiʒt* · schuld attely bi *siʒt*

490-1, *wise* and *nyce*

563-4, *newe* and *shewe;*

so the rimes must, I think, be considered as an inadvertence on the part of the poet, and not as an intended embellishment.

CHARACTER OF THE MS.

The manuscript is neatly written in a handwriting of about 1460; and seemingly with few, if any, errors. At first sight the letter Thorn appears to be used indiscriminately for Th, but I find that it is *never* used at the beginning of a line, and *never* at the end of a word, whether it be written, for example, *serveth*, or *servethe*. The Th is used in proper names; and the few other cases where it is found are, with one exception (thykke), where the sound occurs before the vowel *e*. Thus Sythen, Murther, Ferther, Therefore, and Beetheth, are thus spelt whenever they are found; and Thefe is only once spelt þefe.

The ʒ is constantly used, representing *gh* in the middle of words and *y* at the beginning.

In most cases where we write *er* in our modern speech, and especially in word-endings, such as *after, water, together*, &c., the scribe uses a contraction representing *ur*, making the words *aftur, watur*, &c.

Where the double *l* is crossed (ƚƚ), a final *e* has been assumed.

DATE AND DIALECT OF THE POEM.

The date of our poem in its present form appears to be the latter end of the 14th century; and the dialect in which it is written is Midland, and probably East Midland, as will be seen by the following observations.

The present indicative plurals of regular verbs end everywhere in *-en.* There appears to be an exception to this in l. 72, 'hem that it *deservethe;*' but 'hem' may either be miswritten for 'her;' or else perhaps it is used indeterminately, as 'they' and 'them' are sometimes used now-a-days.

It is not West Midland; for the 3rd sing. indic. almost universally ends in *-eth;* the only exceptions being '*lykes*' in l. 134; '*wendes*' in ll. 155 and 178; '*launces*' in l. 323, and '*formerknes*' in l. 362, though this last (see the note on the line) is a doubtful instance. Robert of Brunne also uses this termination in *-es;* but always, apparently, for the sake of the rime.

The second person sing. indic. ends in *-est;* excepting the word '*fyndes*' in l. 305. 'Thou *were*' is used in lines 236-7.

In many instances the *e* final is omitted in the past tense of weak verbs; as, delyvered, 155 and 178; graunted, 189 and 246. See also ll. 18, 24, 28, 39, 62, 91, 107, 108, 255, 275, 281, and 339.

There are some terminations in *-eth*, used instead of *-ed* for the perfect participles of regular verbs. See ll. 78, 175, 200, 209, 310.

The plurals of nouns end almost universally in *-es;* the only exceptions being *lond-is*, l. 16, *lyon-ys*, l. 214, and *bell-ys*, l. 272 (which are perhaps only variations made by the copyist); *dom-us*, l. 91; and *chylderen*, ll. 20 and 82.

Fader is uninflected in the possessive case, l. 203. The other genitives are in *-es*.

Some nouns of time and measure are uninflected in the plural; as ȝere, l. 89, 243 (we say now 'a two-*year*-old colt'), and *myle*, l. 95 (we say now 'it is a *two-mile* course').

Of the personal pronouns—

I is always used, and not *Ic*.

All people alike, king and peasant, *Thou* and *Thee* one another, without the distinction of rank, such as is shown in William of Palerne, by the use of *Ye* and *You*. In one instance, l. 26, the King addresses the Queen as *Ye*. *Hym* is the objective singular, and *Hem* (in one instance *Ham*, probably for þam—a Northern form) the plural : *Them* is never used.

She is the 3rd person fem. nominative, and *Here* or *Her* objective, the latter being used 8 times in the poem, and the former 9.

Hit and *It* are used about equally, the latter rather more frequently. *They* is always used in the plural.

The possessive pronoun of the 3rd person feminine, is *Her* or *Here*. In the plural of all genders it is *Here*, and once *Her*.

The negative form of the verb To Be is once used in *Nere* = ne were, l. 3.

The imperfect participles end always in *-ynge*.

This is contrary to early Midland usage, and seems to show that the dialect here employed must have been spoken in the Southern part of the East Midland district, *-inge* being a Southern form, though it is used in another East Midland book, 'Body and Soul,' l. 396 [brennynge], and by Robert of Brunne 'Handlyng Synne;' and by Chaucer. But as the peculiarities of each dialect were no doubt always understood by the neighbours on the borders of the several districts, and by degrees became naturalized beyond their ancient limits; so probably at the time when the Cheualere Assigne was written, the Southern and Midland dialects at least were beginning to blend and form a common language.

One peculiarity in this author's style is a strange mixing of past and present tenses ; i. e. in the same sentence he constantly, as does also Chaucer sometimes, uses the historical present, and the perfect. Thus in l. 229,

'The chylde *stryketh* hym to, & *toke* hym by þe brydelle.'

See also lines 63, 115-16, 151, 155, 173, 178, 190, 221, 267, 332, 341, 355, 361-2, and 365.

Mr Morris writes, 'The Dialect in its *present form* is East Midland. But as we do not find [other] East Midland writers adopting alliterative measure in the 14th century, I am inclined to think that the original English text was written in the N. or N.W. of England, and that the present copy is a mere modified transcript. This theory accounts for the *es's* in the 3rd person [sing.], which are not required for the rime, and may be forms belonging to the earlier copy, and unaltered by the later scribe.'

I have to thank Mr Morris, Mr Skeat, and Mr Furnivall for their kind suggestions during the progress of my work, and I must make also my acknowledgments to Mr Brock for his faultless transcript.

Although, therefore, I suppose that, from their uncertain character, the dialect or grammatical peculiarities of this poem are not of any particular value in the history of the language, yet as it is at any rate a contribution to that history, and as I think that whatever is worth doing at all, is worth doing thoroughly, I have made the Glossary as copious and accurate as I could. Besides, there is some spirit and vigour in the Poem itself; and I hope the reading of the little book may be as entertaining to the members of the Early English Text Society, as the editing of it has been to me.

H. H. G.

POSTSCRIPT TO THE PREFACE

OF THE

Chevelere Assigne.

IN the foregoing Preface I have given a short account of the story told in the cycle of Lays, of which the "Chevalier Assigne" (Helyas) forms a part, and to which it gives a name, but it may be well that I should describe more precisely the component parts of the Cycle in question, and fix the place which it holds in the list of Rhapsodies commemorating the deeds of the ancient heroes of romance.

These songs of the Troubadours—the Homers of the Middle Ages—were called *Chansons de Geste* (historic songs), and told of the exploits of Charlemagne and his mighty men, of William of Orange (otherwise called William with the Short Nose), of the four sons of Aymon; of Arthur and his knights; of Jerusalem and its fortunes, and of the heroes who fought in the Crusades for its recovery from the enemies of the Faith.

The Lives or Acts of the various heroes commemorated form severally branches of the principal epic cycle under which they are ranged, whether of Charlemagne, of the Round Table, or of that with which we are here concerned, and which was called "the Cycle of the knight of the Swan," or else "the Cycle of Godfrey of Boulogne." Under this latter cycle are grouped five lays, properly belonging to it, forming what we may call a Godofrediad, since it is all, or almost all, written to Godfrey's glory, beginning with the miraculous birth of his ancestor Helyas, and ending with his crowning deed, the capture of Jerusalem.

These five lays are,

I. The CHANSON D'ANTIOCHE, treating of the Voyage of Peter the hermit, the entry of the Crusaders into Palestine, and the conquest of Antioch. It is the earliest in point of composition, and appears to have been the germ and nucleus of the other members of the cycle, as well as a model for the songs of other Troubadours. From their writings we gather that it was current early in the 12th century. To the Chevalier William of Bechada, who wrote before 1137, to William, Count of Poitiers, and to Richard the pilgrim, himself present at the first Crusade, has the honour of its composition been attributed; but we know it only in the more modern form given to it by the Troubadour Graindor of Douai in 1268. It was edited in 1848, by M. Paulin Paris.

II. THE CHANSON DE JERUSALEM, describing the conquest of the Holy City, was founded on the lay of Richard the pilgrim; but has come down to us only in the revision of Graindor (published by M. Hippeau in 1868), who in arranging anew this and the preceding Geste, incorporated with them

III. The Lay of THE CAPTIVES (*Chetifs*), a work of a later period in the same century, but founded, so M. Paulin Paris thinks, on a Chanson of William IX, Count of Poitiers, who returned to his country in 1102, one of the few survivors of a disastrous expedition to the East, of which he was the leader after the entry of the crusaders into Jerusalem.

IV. The Lay of HELYAS, being the story of the Knight of the Swan himself; the beginning of which, as quoted below, shows that this branch at least of the cycle was of later date than the cycle of Arthur. It appears to have been written about 1190.

V. LES ENFANCES DE GODEFFROY, the earlier form of which seems to have been written by a nameless Troubadour in the first part of the 12th century; and the later version by one RENAUD or RENAX, in the later years of the same, or early in the succeeding, century.

The French poem to which I referred in the Preface, as contained in the "Shrewsbury book" (Royal. 15 E vj in the British Museum), appears to be an amalgamation into one Chanson of all the five branches of this cycle.

It differs very considerably from the version of the Chanson extant in the MSS. consulted by M. Paris, as is evident from a comparison of the British Museum MS. with the extracts given by him in the 22nd volume of the *Histoire Litteraire de la France.* Many lines are the same, many slightly altered, and many lines, and even long passages, are omitted in one and find a place in the other. These variations no doubt arise from the handing down the lays from bard to bard, by oral tradition in a great measure; each singer drawing from his imagination to supply any lack in his memory; and each probably, by dictation to some scribe, perpetuating his variations, whether of matter or dialect, in his own province or neighbourhood.

Take, for example, the first five lines of the poem (after the two quoted on p. ii. in the note), which in the Paris MS. stand as

> Teus i a qui vous cantent de la Reonde Table,
> Des manteaux anjoulés, de samis et de sable ;
> Mais jou ne vous voel dire ne mensonge ne fable.
> En escrist la fist la bone dame Orable
> Dedens les murs d'Orange la fort cité mirable ;

and in the London MS. as

> Telȝ y a qui nous chantent de la Ronde table,
> Des manteaulx angolés, de samin et de sable ;
> Mais je ne vous diray ne menconge ne flabe ; [*sic*]
> Quer il est en ystoire, cest chose veritable,
> En escript le fist mettre la bonne dame orable.

Again, the description of the birth of the children occupies but four lines in the MS. quoted by M. Paris :

> Au naistre des enfans set fées y avoit
> Qui les enfans faerent, si com lor avenroit
> Et quant l'uns des enfans après l'autre nascoit
> Au col une caïne de blanc argent avoit ;

but the Shrewsbury book gives eight to them and Matabrune :

> Au naistre des enfans nulle femme ny avoit
> Fors une vielle dame qui eu Dieu pou creoit
> Mere estoit au *Seigneu*r, la royne fort hayoit,
> A amasser avoir tout son penser estoit.
> La dame se delivre a paine et a destroit ;
> L'un enfant à pres lautre si com dieu le voulloit,

> Si com l'un enfant à pres lautre naissoit,
> Au col une chaine de fin argent avoit.

The account of the sorrowful leavetaking of Helyas and his Beatrice is thus ended in the Paris and London MS. respectively—

> Là plorent vavassor et prince et castelain,
> Oncques n'en ot à Blaives si grant duel por Audain,
> Quant fut morte de duel por son cousin germain.
>
> Lors pleurent prevost et chastelain,
> Dames et pucelle, nobleȝ et vilain;
> Plus de c se pasmerent sur le terrain.

The name Helyas (in its various forms of Helias, Helius, Helis or Elis, Elias, and Salvius) is derived by Mr Baring-Gould from the Keltic Ala, Eala, Ealadh, a Swan. See his "Curious Myths of the Middle Ages" (2nd Series, 1868), which contains an interesting treatise on the Legend of the Knight of the Swan.

In further illustration of my subject I will mention that the museum of the *Maison de Cluny* at Paris contains an ivory casket, the carvings on which represent a part of the story of our book. According to M. Francisque Michel, its date is of the end of the 13th or beginning of the 14th century. It is not nearly so full in its details as the Tyntesfield casket, but is interesting as giving additional evidence of the popularity of the legend of the CHEVALIER AU CYGNE.

H. H. GIBBS.

2 *Sept.*, 1870.

.;. CHEUELERE .;. ASSIGNE .;.

[*Cotton MS. Caligula* A. ii., *fol.* 125 *b.*]

¶ Alle weldynge god · whenne it is his wylle,   God Almighty guards us,
Wele he wereth his · werke with his owne honde :
For ofte harmes were hente · þat helpe we ne my3te ;
Nere þe hy3nes of hym · þat lengeth in heuene.   4
For this I saye by a lorde · was lente in an yle,   as we see by the story of King Oryens,
That was kalled lyor · a londe by hym selfe.
The kynge hette oryens · as þe book tellethe ;
And his qwene bewtrys · þat bry3t was & shene :   8   and Beatrice his queen, and his mother Matabryne.
¶ His moder hy3te Matabryne · þat made moche sorwe ;
For she sette her affye · in Sathanas of helle.
This was chefe of þe kynde · of cheualere assygne ;
And whenne þey sholde in-to a place · it seyth fulle wele where,   12
Sythen aftur his lykynge · dwellede he þere,
Withe his owne qwene · þat he loue my3te :
But alle in langour he laye · for lofe of here one,
That he hadde no chylde · to cheuenne his londis ;   16   He had no child to succeed him,
¶ But to be lordeles of his · whenne he þe lyf lafte :
And þat honged in his herte · I heete þe for sothe.   which was a grief.

    Line 5. See note on l. 23.
    6. lyor. In the French poem it is *Lilefort*, and in Copland also.
    7—9. The King is called *Oriant* in the French version, and the Queen *Bietrix*, and the King's mother *Matebrune*.
    11. 'This' must mean 'this King.'
    12. I cannot make sense of this line. 'Sholde' = should go, and 'it' means the book.
    18. honged in his herte = weighed upon his mind.

THE QUEEN BEARS SEVEN AT A BIRTH.

The King and the Queen, talking on the wall, see beneath them a woman with her twins,

As þey wente vp-on a walle · pleynge hem one,
Bothe þe kynge & þe qwene · hem selfen to-gedere : 20
The kynge loked a-downe · & by-helde vnder,
And seyȝ a pore womman · at þe ȝate Sytte,
Withe two chylderen her by-fore · were borne at a byrthe ;

whereat he weeps. And he turned hym þenne · & teres lette he falle. 24
¶ Sythen sykede he on-hyȝe · & to þe qwene sayde,
'Se ȝe þe ȝonder pore womman · how þat she is pyned
Withe twynlenges two · & þat dare I my hedde wedde.'

The Queen says she disbelieves in twins. Each must have a father.

The qwene nykked hym with nay · & seyde 'it is not to leue : 28
Oon manne for oon chylde · & two wymmen for tweyne ;
Or ellis hit were vnsemelye þynge · as me wolde þenke,
But eche chylde hadde a fader · how manye so þer were.'

The King rebukes her,

The kynge rebukede here for her worþes ryȝte þere ; 32
¶ And whenne it drowȝ towarde þe nyȝte · þey wenten to bedde ;

and at night begets on her reasonably many children,

He gette on here þat same nyȝte · resonabullye manye.
The kynge was witty · whenne he wysste her with chylde,
And þankede lowely our lorde · of his loue & his sonde. 36

---

19. walle. The French has '*tour*.'
23. Chaucer frequently omits the relative, as is done here.
26. 'is pyned' must mean 'has travailed,' or been in pain.
28. it is not to leue. The edition of 1820 has *lene*. In the French it is *vous parlez de neant*.
29. This means, 'One man can beget but one child, nor can one woman have more than one at a time by the same man. Two honestly-begotten children must needs have two mothers.' Twins were once thought to reflect on the mother's chastity.
The French poem has

Sa deux hommes ne sest livree charnellement.
31. how manye so = howso[ever] many.
32. ryȝte there = On the spot.
33 & 37. drowȝ and drowȝe. 'The correct form is *drow*.'—R. Morris.
34. He gette, &c. It is printed *gotte* in the Roxb. ed., but the word is plainly *gette* in the MS. The French has

*Engendra le seigneur en la dame vaillant
vij enfans celle nuit en ung engendrement.*

But whenne it drowȝe to þe tyme · she shulde be de-
  lyuered,
Ther moste no womman come her nere · but she þat
  was cursed,
His moder matabryne · þat cawsed moche sorowe;
For she thowȝte to do þat byrthe · to a fowle ende. 40
¶ Whenne god wolde þey were borne · þenne browȝte
  she to honde
Sex semelye sonnes · & a dowȝter þe seueneth,   *to wit, six sons and a daughter,*

.;. MATABRYNE. .;.   [Fol. 126.]

Alle safe & alle sounde · & a seluer cheyne   *with silver chains about their necks.*
Eche on of hem hadde · a-bowte his swete swyre. 44
And she lefte hem out · & leyde hem in a cowche;
And þenne she sente aftur a man · þat markus was   *But Matabryne sends for her man Marcus,*
  called,
That hadde serued her-selueñ · skylfully longe:
He was trewe of his feyth · & loth for to tryfulle; 48
¶ She knewe hym for swych · & triste hym þe better;
And seyde, 'þou moste kepe counselle · & helpe what
  þou may:
The fyrste grymme watur · þat þou to comeste, 51   *and bids him drown the children.*
Looke þou caste hem þer-In · & lete hym forthe slyppe:
Sythen seche to þe courte · as þou nowȝte hadde sene,
And þou shalt lyke fulle wele · yf þou may lyfe aftur.'

39. 'þat cawsed moche sorowe.' These words, and 'the cursede man in his feyth,' are, like the Homeric ποδας ωκυς and ποιμενα λαων, applied as a sort of verse-tag to fill up the line, and serve as constant epithets respectively to Matabryne and Malkedras.
40. do.. to a fowle ende. See l. 138. As in Shakespere, Much Ado about Nothing, V. 3: '*Done* to death with slanderous tongues.'
45. lefte = lifted.
46. Markus, called *Marques* and *Marcon* in the French poem.
49. knewe, should be *knew;* the *e* is superfluous; but it is so in the MS.

49. swych. Wrongly printed *swyth* in the Roxb. ed.
triste. Wrongly printed *tristed*, in the same, moste; the *e* is superfluous.
50. kepe counselle = be secret.
52. hym for *hem*.
53. seche = betake thyself. Comp. Ezekiel xiv. 10, 'him that seeketh unto him.'
54. lyke full wele = be well-liking = prosper. Comp. 'fat and well-liking,' Ps. xcii. 13; 'worse-liking,' Daniel i. 10. 'I believe the original construction was, "And it shal like þe ful wel" = and it shall please thee full well. See l. 134.'—R. Morris.

Marcus grieves, but dares not disobey.	Whenne he herde þat tale · hym rewede þe tyme;
But he durste not werne · what þe qwene wolde. 56
¶ The kynge lay in langour · sum gladdenes to here;
But þe fyrste tale þat he herde · were tydynges febulle,
Whenne his moder matabryne · browȝte hym tydynge.
At a chamber dore · as she forthe sowȝte, 60
She takes seven whelps,	Seuenne whelpes she sawe · sowkynge þe damme,
And she kawȝte out a knyfe · & kylled þe bycche;
She caste her þenne in a pytte · & takethe þe welpes,
And sythen come byfore þe kynge · & vp on-hyȝe she seyde, 64
and shows 'em to the King as the Queen's offspring, and bids him have her burnt.	¶ 'Sone paye þe with þy qwene · & se of her berthe.'
Thenne syketh þe kynge · & gynnythe to morne,
And wente wele it were sothe · alle þat she seyde.
Thenne she seyde, 'lette brenne her a-none · for þat is þe beste.' 68
He refuses.	'Dame, she is my wedded wyfe · fulle trewe as I wene,
As I haue holde her er þis · our lorde so me helpe!'
She vituperates.	'A, kowarde of kynde,' quod she · '& combred wrecche!
Wolt þou werne wrake · to hem þat hit deseruethe?'
He says, 'Stow her where thou wilt, so that I see it not.'	¶ 'Dame, þanne take here þy selfe · & sette her wher þe lykethe, 73
So þat I se hit noȝte · what may I seye elles?'
She falls foul of the Queen,	Thenne she wente her forthe · þat god shalle confounde,
To þat febulle þer she laye · & felly she bygynnethe, 76
And seyde, 'a-ryse wrecched qwene · & reste þe her no lengur;
Thow hast by-gylethe my sone · it shalle þe werke sorowe:
Bothe howndes & men · haue hadde þe a wylle:
Thow shalt to prisoun fyrste · & be brente aftur.' 80

60. sowȝte. See note on l. 53.
64. come. The correct form is com.
on-hyȝe = aloud.
68. lette brenne her = have her burnt.
72. deserueth. As to this termination in -eth, see Preface, p. xvi.
75. See note on l. 190.
78. by-gylethe. The final e is unnecessary; but there is a contraction representing it in the MS.

THE QUEEN IMPRISONED. THE CHILDREN ARE EXPOSED. 5

¶ Thenne shrykede þe ȝonge qwene · & vp on hyȝ cryethe, *and, in spite of her moans,*
' A, lady,' she seyde · ' where ar my lefe chylderen ? '
Whenne she myssede hem þer · grete mone she made.
By þat come tytlye · tyrauntes tweyne, 84
And by þe byddynge of matabryne · a-non þey her hente,
And in a dymme prysoun · þey slongen here deepe, *[Fol. 126 b.] has her thrown*
And leyde a lokke on þe dore · & leuen here þere : 87 *into prison,*
Mete þey caste here a-downe · & more god sendethe. *where she lies eleven years.*
¶ And þus þe lady lyuede þere · elleuen ȝere,
And mony a fayre orysoun · vn-to þe fader made,
That saued Susanne fro sorowefulle domus · [her] to saue als. *But God, who saved Susanna, hears her prayer also.*
Now leue we þis lady in langour & pyne, 92
And turne aȝeyne to our tale · towarde þese chylderen,
And to þe man markus · þat murther hem sholde ;
How he wente þorow a foreste · fowre longe myle, *Marcus takes the children to drown them.*
Thylle he come to a watur · þer he hem shulde in drowne ; 96
¶ And þer he keste vp þe clothe · to knowe hem bettur,
And þey ley & lowȝe on hym · louelye alle at ones : *But they look on him in lovely*
' He þat lendethe wit,' quod he · ' leyne me wyth sorowe, *wise,*
If I drowne ȝou to day · thowghe my deth be nyȝe.' 100 *and he won't,*
Thenne he leyde hem adowne · lappedde in þe mantelle, *but leaves them*
And lappede hem, & hylyde hem · & hadde moche rewthe, *all wrapped in a mantle, and commends them to Christ.*
That swyche a barmeteme as þat · shulde so be-tyde.
Thenne he takethe hem to criste · & aȝeyne turnethe. 104

---

81. See note on l. 64.
84. By þat = by that time, then.
tyrauntes. The French poem has *Sers* (serfs).
86. slongen. Roxb. ed. has *flongen*, which is an error of transcription.
90. This particular orison, with Susanna for its example, finds a place in the French poem, not at this point, but during the procession from the city to the place of burning, Mata-

bryne's remark thereon being '*ça ne vault ung bouton.*'
91. domus. This *might* be a mis-writing for ' *dom* (= doom) *us*,' as the former edition reads it ; but it is, no doubt, a plural in *us*, the word *her* having slipped out.
99. wit. Wrongly printed w*th* in the former edition.
103. swyche. See note on l. 49.

¶ But sone þe mantelle was vn-do · with mengynge of
  her legges ;
They cryedde vp on-hyȝe · with a dolefulle steuenne,
They chyuered for colde · as cheuerynge chyldreñ,

A hermit hears them sob,
They ȝoskened, & cryde out · & þat a man herde, 108
An holy hermyte was by · & towarde hem cometh*e* :
Whenne he come by-tore hem · on knees þenne he felle,

and cries to Christ for succour;
And cryede ofte vpon cryste · for somme sokour hym
  to sende,
If any lyfe were hem lente · in þis worlde lengur. 112

a hind comes and suckles them ;
¶ Thenne an hynde kome fro þe woode · rennynge fulle
  swyfte,
And felle be-fore hem adowñe · þey drowȝe to þe
  pappes ;
The heremyte prowde was þer-of · & putte hem to
  sowke :

and the hermit takes them home and tends them.
Sethen taketh he hem vp · & þe hynde folowethe, 116
And she kepte hem þere · whylle our lorde wolde.
Thus he noryscheth hem vp · & criste hem helpe send-
  ethe.
Of sadde leues of þe wode · wrowȝte he hem wedes.

Malkedras the Forester passes and sees them,
Malkedras þe fostere · þe fende mote hym haue, 120
¶ That cursedde man for his feythe · he come þer þey
  wereñ,
And was ware in his syȝte · syker of þe chyldren ;
He turnede aȝeyn to þe courte · & tolde of þe chaunce,

tells Matabryne,
And menede byfore matabryne · how mony þer were. 124
' And more merueyle þenne þat · Dame, a seluere cheyne
Eche on of hem hath · abowte here swyre.'
She seyde, 'holde þy wordes in chaste · þat none skape
  ferther ;
I wylle soone aske hym · þat hath me betrayed.' 128

119. sadde leues of þe wode. Fr. *feuilles de loriers.*
120. Malkedras is called in the French MS. *Malquarrez* and *Mauquarre.*
124. menede. Wrongly printed *meuede* in the Roxb. ed.
127. holde thy wordes in chaste = be silent.

HE ROBS SIX OF THEIR SILVER CHAINS. THEY BECOME SWANS.

¶ Thenne she sente aftur markus · þat murther hem sholde ; who questions Marcus,
And askede hym, in good feythe · what felle of þe chyldren :
Whenne she hym asked hadde · he seyde, 'here þe sothe;
Dame, on a ryueres banke · lapped in my mantelle, 132 and, hearing the truth, has his eyes put out;
I lafte hem lyynge there · leue þou for sothe :
I myȝte not drowne hem for dole · do what þe lykes.'
Thenne she made here alle preste · & (putt) out bothe hys yen.
Moche mone was therfore · but no man wyte moste. 136
¶ 'Wende þou aȝeyne malkedras · & gete me þe cheynes, sends Malkedras to take the chains, and slay the children.
And withe þe dynte of þy swerde · do hem to dethe ;
And I shalle do þe swych a turne · & þou þe tyte hyȝe,
That þe shalle lyke ryȝte wele · þe terme of þy lyue.' 140
Thenne þe hatefulle thefe · hyed hym fulle faste,
The cursede man in his feythe · come þer þey were.
By þenne was þe hermyte go in-to þe wode · & on of þe children, He finds but six, one being away with the hermit.
For to seke mete · for þe other sex, 144
¶ Whyles þe cursed man · asseylde þe other :
And he out withe his swerde · & smote of þe cheynes. He smites off the chains; and the children change into swans.
They stoden alle stylle · for stere þey ne durste ;
And whenne þe cheynes felle hem fro · þey flowen vp swannes 148
To þe ryuere by-syde · withe a rewfulle steuenne.
And he takethe vp þe cheynes · & to þe cowrte turnethe,
And come by-fore þe qwene · & here hem bytakethe :
Thenne she toke hem in honde · & heelde ham fulle stylle ; 152
¶ She sente aftur a golde-smyȝte · to forge here a cowpe ;

---

133. leue. Wrongly printed *lene* in the edition of 1820.
135. The Roxb. ed. omits *putt*, which has been added in the margin of the MS. by the original scribe.
138. do. See note on l. 40.
140. See note on l. 54.

(CHEV. ASSIGNE)

<small>The old Queen gives the chains to a goldsmith to make a cup of.</small>

And whenne þe man was comen · þenne was þe qwene
blythe,
And delyuered hym his wey3tes · & he from cowrte
wendes :
She badde þe wesselle were made · vpon alle wyse : 156
The goldesmy3th goothe & beetheth hym a fyre · &
brekethe a cheyne,

<small>One chain multiplies so in the melting-pot, that half of one suffices.</small>

And it wexeth in hys honde · & multyplyethe swyde :
He toke þat oþur fyue · & fro þe fyer hem leyde,
And made hollye þe cuppe · of haluendelle þe sixte. 160
¶ And whenne it drow3e to þe ny3te · he wendethe to
bedde,

<small>The goldsmith tells his wife, and asks her counsel.</small>

And thus he seythe to his wyfe · in sawe as I telle.
'The olde qwene at þe courte · hathe me bytaken
Six cheynes in honde · & wolde haue a cowpe ; 164
And I breke me a cheyne · & halfe leyde in þe fyer,
And it wexedde in my honde · & wellede so faste,
That I toke þe oþur fyve · & fro þe fyer caste,
And haue made hollye þe cuppe · of haluendele þe
sixte.' 168

<small>She says, 'Keep the rest! The Queen has full weight. What would she have more?'
[Fol. 127 b.]</small>

¶ ' I rede þe,' quod his wyfe · ' to holden hem stylle ;
Hit is þorowe þe werke of god · or þey be wronge
wonnen ;
For whenne here mesure is made · what may she aske
more ?' 171
And he dedde as she badde · & buskede hym at morwe ;

<small>He gives the old Queen the cup and the half chain.</small>

He come by-fore þe qwene · & bytaketh here þe cowpe,
And she toke it in honde · & kepte hit fulle clene.
'Nowe lefte ther ony ouur vn-werkethe · by þe better
trowthe ?'
And he recheth her forth · haluendele a cheyne : 176

---

162. The conversation between the goldsmith and his wife is much longer and more dramatic in our poem than in the French.
170. þorowe. Wrongly printed *Thōwe* in the Roxb. ed.
170. wronge wonnen = wrongly (i. e. wrongfully) acquired.
176. recheth. Misprinted *recketh*. forth. Misprinted *ferth* in the Roxb. ed.

¶ And she raw3te hit hym a3eyne · & seyde she ne *She gives him the half chain and his pay.*
   row3te;
But delyuered hym his seruyse · & he out of cowrte
   wendes.
'The curteynesse of criste,' quod she · 'be with þese
   oþur cheynes!   179
They be delyuered out of þis worlde · were þe moder eke,
Thenne hadde I þis londe · hollye to myne wylle :
Now alle wyles shalle fayle · but I here dethe werke.'
At morn she come byfore þe kynge · & by ganne fulle *She scolds the King for leaving his Queen so long unburnt,*
   keene;   183
'Moche of þis worlde sonne · wondrethe on þe altone,
¶ That thy qwene is vnbrente · so meruelows longe,
That hath serued þe dethe · if þou here dome wyste :
Lette sommene þy folke · vpon eche a syde, *and bids him summon his folk.*
That þey bene at þy sy3te · þe .xj. day assygned.' 188
And he here graunted þat · withe a grymme herte; *He grieves; but grants it.*
And she wendeth here adown · & lette hem a-none
   warne.
The ny3te byfore þe day · þat þe lady shulde brenne, *The night before the burning comes an angel to the hermit.*
An Angelle come to þe hermyte · & askede if he slepte:
¶ The angelle seyde, 'criste sendeth þe worde · of þese
   six chyldren;   193
And for þe sauynge of hem · þanke þou haste seruethe :
They were þe kynges Oriens · wytte þou for sothe,

179. '*Puis dist entre ses dens assez
   bassetement
Bien suis de ceulx delivre alez
   sont voirement
Se leur mere estoit arse ne me
   chauldroit neant.*
And then,' she continues, 'by my en-
chantments I will cause that my son
never marries again, and so I shall
have all the land at my command.'
   186. serued. In the Roxb. ed. this
is erroneously printed *dyserved*.
   if thou here dome wyste = if thou
knewest what her sentence ought to be.
   190. wendeth here. 'wend' is here
used reflexively as 'went' is in l. 75,

and 'hy3e' in l. 141, after the French
s'en *alla*. Comp. Shaksp. 2 Gent. of
Ver. IV. 4: 'I .. goes *me* to the fellow.' The phrase in the text seems
to make it more probable that this *me*
is the personal, and not the indeter-
minate pronoun.
   194. þanke þou haste seruethe =
thou hast deserved thanks. The final
e is too much. See note on l. 78.
   195. They were the kynges Oriens =
They were [the children] of the King
Oriens. This expression is not unlike
that in Wm. of Palerne, l. 5437 : þem-
perours moder Williám.

Tells him that the six swan-children are sons of Oryens and Beatrice.	By his wyfe Betryce · she bere hem at ones,	196

                For a worde on þe walle · þat she wronge seyde;
                And ȝonder in þe ryuer · swymmen þey swannes;
                Sythen Malkedras þe forsworn þefe · byrafte hem her
                    cheynes:

But that Christ formed the other child to fight for his mother.
                And criste hath formeth þis chylde · to fyȝte for his
                    moder.'   200

                ¶ 'Oo-lyuynge god þat dwellest in heuene' · quod þe
                    hermyte þanne,

'How can this be?'
                'How sholde he serue for suche a þynge · þat neuur
                    none syȝe?'

'Take him to Court and have him christened Enyas.'
                'Go brynge hym to his fader courte · & loke þat he be
                    cristened;   203

                And kalle hym Enyas to name · for awȝte þat may be-falle,
                Ryȝte by þe mydday · to redresse his moder;
                For goddes wylle moste be fulfylde · & þou most forthe
                    wende.'

                The heremyte wakynge lay · & thowȝte on his wordes:
                Soone whenne þe day come · to þe chylde he seyde, 208

The hermit tells the child what he is to do, what a mother is, [Fol. 128.]
                ¶ 'Criste hath formeth þe sone · to fyȝte for þy moder.'
                He asskede hymm þanne · what was a moder.
                'A womman þat bare þe to man · sonne, & of her reredde:'
                'Ȝe, kanste þou, fader, enforme me · how þat I shalle
                    fyȝte?'   212
                'Vpon a hors,' seyde þe heremyte · 'as I haue herde seye.'

---

201. Oo. Wrongly printed *To* in the former edition. Oo-lyuynge = ever-living.

202. þynge. Wrongly printed *ȝnge* in the former edition.

204. Enyas; not *Ænyas*, as in the old edition. The French poem has *Elyas* or *Helyas*, which latter is the name given him in the English prose Romance.

A line seems to be omitted between 204 and 205, such as
    'Let hym cair to þe court · þer þe
        kynge dwellethe.'

210. The conversation between the hermit and the child is more full in the English than in the French poem.

211. A very cramped line. 'A woman that bare thee to man, [my] son; and [thou wast] by her reared.'

'It means, "bare thee so that thou becamest a man." Such is the regular idiom; [God] *wrouȝt me to man* = formed thee so that thou becamest a man, fashioned thee in man's shape; occurs in Piers Plowman, A. Pass. i. 1. 80.'—W. W. S.

'*Beau filz cest une femme quen ses flans te porta.*'

HE MEETS THE PROCESSION, AND ACCOSTS THE KING.

'What beste is þat?' quod þe chylde · 'lyonys wylde? <small>and what a horse,</small>
Or elles wode? or watur' · quod þe chylde panne. <small>on which he is to fight.</small>
'I seyȝe neuur none,' quod þe hermyte · 'but by þe mater
   of bokes: 216
¶ They seyn he hath a feyre hedde · & fowre lymes hye;
And also he is a frely beeste · for-thy he man seruethe.'
'Go we forthe, fader,' quod þe childe 'vpon goddes halfe!' <small>The child is willing, and they</small>
The grypte eyþur a staffe in here honde · & on here wey <small>go forth on their way.</small>
   strawȝte. 220
Whenne þe heremyte hym lafte · an angelle hym suwethe, <small>The hermit leaves the child,</small>
Euur to rede þe chylde · vpon his ryȝte sholder. <small>and an angel goes with him and counsels him.</small>
Thenne he seeth in a felde · folke gaderynge faste,
And a hyȝ fyre was þer bette · þat þe qwene sholde in <small>The child sees a great crowd and</small>
   brenne, 224 <small>a fire kindled in a field,</small>
¶ And noyse was in þe cyte · felly lowde, <small>and a great troop bringing the</small>
With trumpes & tabers · whenne þey here vp token; <small>Queen from the city.</small>
The olde qwene at here bakke · betynge fulle faste;
The kynge come rydynge a-fore · a forlonge & more; 228 <small>The King rides in front.</small>
The chylde stryketh hym to · & toke hym by þe brydelle:
'What man arte þou?' quod þe chylde · '& who is þat <small>'Who art thou? and who are these?' quoth the child.</small>
   þe svethe?'

---

215. Or else [a] wood[-beast], or [a] water[-beast]?
219. Comp. William of Palerne, l. 2803, 'Go we now on goddes halve.'
220. The grypte eyþur = They each seized.
221. suwethe. The Roxb. editor has mistaken this for *seemeth*.
221-2. rede. Here we find *ride* in the former edition; but besides that it is not so written, the French original shows that it must be as in the text. This incident of the angel does not find its place here, in the French poem. There, it is when the child accosts the King that the author says,—
   Homme fol et sauvaige a merveilles
     sembloit
   Lange a dieu le pere sur lespaule
     seoit
   Que ce quil devoit dire trop bien lui
     enseignoit.

224. brenne. The final *e* is illegible, being obliterated by a blot of ink.
bette. Comp. Sir Aldingar, l. 53 (Percy folio, vol. i. p. 168), 'And fayre fyer there shalbe *bette*.'
227. *A tant est Matebrune qui*
   a-maine a grant cris
   Batant la bonne dame qui eust nom
   Bietrix.
230. Here in the French poem follows,
   '*Le roy . . .*
   Voulentiers en eust ris mais trop
     dolent estoit.'
He then asks the child what his own name is; and he answers that he has no name, except that with the hermit his name has been always Beau filz. Comp. Libius Disconius, ll. 25—30 and 62—66. Percy folio, vol. ii. p. 416 and 418.

The King answers, and tells the story.	'I am þe kynge of þis londe · & oryens am kalled, And þe ȝondur is my qwene · betryce she hette, 232 ¶ In þe ȝondere balowe fyre · is buskedde to brenne; She was sklawnndered on-hyȝe · þat she hadde taken howndes; And ȝyf she hadde so don · here harm were not to charge.'
'Thou dost ill to be led by Matabryne.	'Thenne were þou noȝt ryȝ[t]lye sworne,' quod þe chylde · 'vpon ryȝte Iuge, 236 Whenne þou tokest þe þy crowne · kynge whenne þou made were, To done aftur matabryne · for þenne þou shalt mysfare,
She is fell and false, and shall go to the fiend.	For she is fowle felle & fals · & so she shalle be fownden, And bylefte with þe fend · at here laste ende, 240 ¶ That styked styffe in here brestes · þat wolde þe qwene brenne:
I am but 12 years old, but I will fight for the Queen.'	I am but lytulle & ȝonge,' quod þe chylde · 'leeue þou forsothe, Not but twelfe ȝere olde · euen at þis tyme, And I wolle putte my body · to better & to worse, 244 To fyȝte for þe qwene · with whome þat wronge seythe.'
The King is content.	Thenne graunted þe kynge · & Ioye he bygynnethe, If any helpe were þer-Inne · þat here clensen myȝte.
The old Queen rebukes him.	By þat come þe olde qwene · & badde hym com þenne: 248

233. ȝondere. Misprinted ȝonders in the Roxb. ed.
235. hadde is erroneously printed shadde in the Roxb. ed.
here harm were not to charge = her death would not be a matter of concern to any one. '*Charge*, in Chaucer, = a matter of difficulty, a matter of consideration.'—R. M.
236-7. The French corresponding to this passage is,
Arse! Dieu dist lenfant, fait as folle iugement

Nas pas a droit inge comme roy loyaument.
vpon ryȝte Iuge = [hast not] rightly judged. These words are evidence that the French poem was the original of the English one; our poet having apparently taken the word *Iuge* into his text without translating it.
243. Not but = only. In modern Lancashire, *no but*, or *not but*.
245. with whom [soever it be] that wrong saith [of her].
248. þenne = thence.

¶ 'To speke with suche on as he · þou mayste ryȝth
  lothe thenke.'   249
'A, dame,' quod þe kynge · 'thowȝte ȝe none synne ? *He speaks up for his Queen, and*
Thow haste for-sette þe ȝonge qwene · þou knoweste   *[Fol. 128 b.] tells what the child says.*
  welle þe sothe :
This chylde þat I here speke withe · seyth þat he
  wolle preue   252
That þou nother þy sawes · certeyne be neyther.'
And þenne she lepte to hym · & kawȝte hym by þe   *Matabryne rushes at the child and tears his hair.*
  lokke ;
That þer leued in here honde · heres an hondredde.
'A, by lyuynge god,' quod þe childe · 'þat bydeste in
  heuene,   256
¶ Thy hedde shalle lye on þy lappe · for þy false turnes. *'Thy head shall lie in thy lap!'*
I aske a felawe anone · a freshe knyȝte aftur,   *quoth he. 'Give me a man to fight with!'*
For to fyȝte with me · to dryue owte þe ryȝte.'
'A, boy,' quod she, 'wylt þou so · þou shalt sone
  myskarye ;   260

254. hym, sc. the child. The passage in the French poem is curious, the writer exhibiting the rage of the contending parties by a furious succession of rimes in *-aige*, the Norman pronunciation of *-age*.

  Mere ce dist le roy vous nestes mie saige
  Veez a ung enfant qui bien semble sauvaige
  Qui dit que peche faictes et ennuy et hontaige
  Que vous la dame a tort vous mettez sur putaige
  Quant la vielle lentent a pou quelle nenrage
  Aux cheveulx prent lenfant plus de c. en arrache
  Dieu aide dist lenfant ci a mal a comtaige
  Ceste vielle hideuse a en son corps la raige
  Plus fait a redoubter que mil lyon sauvaige.
  La glorieuse dame en qui dieu print umbraige
  Menvoye en cor vengence de ce villain hontaige ;
  Ce ne me faisoit mie mon pere en lermitaige.
  Tous ceulx qui lont oy huchent en leur langaige
  Ha : roy de orient ne souffrez tel hontaige ;
  Li enfant dit assez par les sains de cartaige.
  Roy tien a lenfant droit bien pert de hault paraige,
  Nulz homs ne puet mieulx dire tant soit de grant langaige,
  Dieu te la envoye pour dire cest messaige.

256. bydeste. *Sic* in MS. 'It is probably thrown in parenthetically, and addressed to God. So in Havelok,
  "Ihesu crist, þat made mone,
  Þine dremes turne to ioye [sone]
  Þat wite þw that sittes in trone."
It is very abrupt, certainly.'—W. W. S. In Havelok also, there is a Thou in the former part of the sentence, but here there is none.

HE IS CHRISTENED ENYAS, AND IS DUBBED KNIGHT.

'Ha! boy! I'll get me a man that shall mar thee.'

'I wylle gete me a man · þat shalle þe sone marre.'
She turneth her þenne to malkedras · & byddyth hym take armes,

She sends Malkedras.

And badde hym bathe his spere · in þe boyes herte:
And he of suche one · gret skorne he þowȝte.   264

An Abbot christens the child Enyas.

¶ An holy abbot was þer-by · & he hym þeder bowethe,
For to cristen þe chylde · frely & feyre;
The abbot maketh hym a fonte · & was his godfader,
The erle of auñthepas · he was another,   268
The countes of salamere · was his godmoder;
They kallede hym Enyas to name · as þe book tellethe:
Mony was þe ryche ȝyfte · þat þey ȝafe hym aftur:

The bells ring of themselves all the fight through, betokening that Christ was well pleased.

Alle þe bellys of þe close · rongen at ones   272
¶ Withe-oute ony mannes helpe · whyle þe fyȝte lasted;
Wherefore þe wyste welle · þat criste was plesed with here dede.
Whenne he was cristened · frely & feyre,

The King dubs Enyas knight.

Aftur, þe kynge dubbede hym knyȝte · as his kynde wolde: 276
Thenne prestly he prayeth þe kynge · þat he hym lene wolde

The King lends him his good steed Feraunce, and armour, and a shield with a cross on it.

An hors with his harnes · & blethelye he hym grauntethe:
Thenne was feraunce fette forthe · þe kynges price stede,
And out of an hyȝe towre · armour þey halenne;   280
¶ And a whyte shelde with a crosse · vpon þe posse honged,
And hit was wryten þer-vpon · þat to enyas hit sholde:

---

261. marre. This is written in the MS. with a long *r* in the second place; and the former editor mistook it for a *y*, and wrote the word *marye*. The word 'miscarrye' in the line above might have undeceived him, for it also has the long *r*, followed by a real *y*.

262. þenne. Printed *thence* in the Roxb. ed.

265. An holy abbot. '*L'Abbe Gautier*,' says the French book.

271. ȝyfte. This is misprinted ȝystc in the 1820 edition.

274. welle. Misprinted *welt* in the other edition.

279. Feraunce is *Ferrant* in the French poem.

281. posse. Perhaps miswritten for *poste*, as Utterson has printed it: it is, however, so written in the MS. Ayenbyte of Inwyt.

282. hit sholde [belong].

HE CONSULTS WITH A KNIGHT OF THE KING'S. 15

And whenne he was armed · to alle his ryȝtes, 283
Thenne prayde he þe kynge · þat he hym lene wolde
Oon of his beste menne · þat he moste truste,
To speke with hym but · a speche whyle. *Enyas takes counsel with a*
A knyȝte kawȝte hym by þe honde · & laddo hym of *Knight whom*
þe rowte: 287 *the King lends him,*
'What beeste is þis,' quod þe childe · 'þat I shalle on
 houe?'

¶ 'Hit is called an hors,' quod þe knyȝte · 'a good & an *and learns what is a horse,*
 abulle.'
'Why etethe he yren?' quod þe chylde · 'wylle he ete
 noȝthe elles?
And what is þat on his bakke · of byrthe, or on *a saddle, a bridle,*
 bounden?' *a hawberk, a helm, a shield, a*
'Nay, þat in his mowthe · men kallen a brydelle, 292 *lance, and a* [Fol. 129.]
And that a sadelle on his bakke · þat þou shalt in *sword; and how to use them.*
 sytte.'
'And what heuy kyrtelle is þis · withe holes so thykke?
And þis holowe [on] on my hede · I may noȝt wele
 here.'
'An helme men kallen þat on · & an hawberke þat
 other.' 296
¶ 'But what broode on is þis on my breste · hit bereth
 adown my nekke.'
'A bryȝte shelde & a sheene · to shylde þe fro strokes.'
'And what longe on is þis · that I shalle vp lyfte?'
'Take þat launce vp in þyn honde · & loke þou hym *'See thou hit him.'*
 hytte; 300

285. truste, pf. of trust; it is *triste* in l. 49.
286. a speche whyle. Comp. Shaksp. Two Gent. of Verona, IV. 3.
287. of = from out of.
288. houe. The Roxb. editor reads *hone*, and takes it to be the O.E. Hon = to hang, but it is doubtless Hove = abide, be.
290. The child puts this question to the King, in the French poem.

291. of byrthe = congenital, born with him, natural.
295. wele. This word is added in the margin in a later hand. It is omitted in the edition of 1820.
holowe = hollow one: the *on* has dropped out, because of the preposition following. See ll. 297, 299.
296. þat other. Misprinted *þe other* in the 1820 edition.

And whenne þat shafte is schyuered · take scharpelye
another.'

'ȝe, what yf grace be · we to grownde wenden?'

'A-ryse vp lyȝtly on þe fete · & reste þe no lengur; 303

And þenne plukke out þy swerde · & pele on hym faste,

¶ Alle-wey eggelynges down · on alle þat þou fyndes;

His ryche helm nor his swerde · rekke þou of neyþur;

Lete þe sharpe of þy swerde · schreden hym smalle.'

'But wolle not he smyte aȝeyne · whenne he feleth
smerte?' 308

'ȝys, I knowe hym fulle wele · bothe kenely & faste:

Euur folowe þou on þe flesh · tylle þou haste hym
fallethe;

And sythen smyte of his heede · I kan sey þe no
furre.'

'Now þou haste tawȝte me,' quod þe childe · 'god I þe
beteche: 312

¶ For now I kan of þe crafte · more þenne I kowthe.'

Thenne þey maden Raunges · & ronnen to-gedere,

That þe speres in here hondes · shyuereden to peces;

And for [to] rennene aȝeyn · men rawȝten hem other, 316

Of balowe tymbere & bygge · þat wolde not breste;

And eyther of hem · so smer[t]lye smote other,

That alle fleye in þe felde · þat on hem was fastened,

And eyther of hem topseyle · tumbledde to þe erthe; 320

¶ Thenne here horses ronnen forth · aftur þe raunges,

Euur feraunce by-forne · & þat other aftur;

Side-notes:
'and if we come to ground?'
'Get up again. Draw thy sword, smite him with the edge, snred him in pieces.'
'But won't he smite again?'
'That will he! never mind! smite off his head!'
They run together, shiver their spears,
smash their armour, and upset each other.
The horses run round the lists.

302. ȝe. Misprinted Se in the edition of 1820.
303. lyȝtly. Misprinted lyȝt in 1820.
305. eggelynges = edgewise. With the edge. The contrary of '*flatlings*.'
307. sharpe = sharp edge.
309. ȝys = yes. Its use here instead of ȝe, as in l. 302, is due to the negative in the question.
310. fallethe = felled.
316. rennene may be *rennenge, sb.*; but more probably the line should be as above, the *to* having been accidentally omitted by the scribe.
320. topseyle. *Sic* in MS. Top = head,—as we say, 'from *top* to toe.' Should it be perhaps 'topteyle'? Comp. Wm. of Palerne, l. 2776:
'Set hire a sad strok so sore in þe necke
þat sche *top ouer tail* tombled ouer þe hacches.'
321. ronnen. Misprinted *rennen* in the Roxb. ed.
322. *Le destrier Elyas va, lautre poursuivant.*

Feraũce launces vp his fete · & lasschethe out his
yeñ :
The fyrste happe, other hele · was þat · þat þe chylde *Feraunce lashes out and blinds the other horse.*
hadde,   324
Whenne þat þe chylde þat hym bare · blente hadde his
fere :
Thenne thei styrte vp on hy · with staloworth shankes, *Enyas and Malkedras start up and draw their swords.*
Pulledde out her swerdes · & smoten to-gedur.
'Kepe þy swerde fro my croyse' · quod cheuelrye *'Beware my cross!'*
assygne :   328
¶ 'I charde not þy croyse,' quod malkedras · 'þe valwe *'I don't care a cherry for your cross!'*
of a cherye ;
For I shalle choppe it fulle smalle · ere þenne þis werke
ende.'
An edder spronge out of his shelde · & in his body *An adder strikes him from out the cross; and a fire thereout blinds him.*
spynnethe ;
A fyre fruscheth out of his croys · & [f]rapte out his
yen :   332
Thenne he stryketh a stroke · Cheualere assygne, *Enyas cuts him down and takes [Fol. 129 b.] off his head.*
Eueñ his sholder in twoo · & dowñ in-to þe herte ;
And he bowethe hym dowñ · & ʒeldethe vp þe lyfe.
'I shalle þe ʒelde,' quod þe chylde · 'ryʒte as þe knyʒte
me tawʒte.'   336

323. yeñ. The transcriber for the Roxb. ed. mistook the curl over the *n* (ñ) for a *d*, as if it was *rd*, and wrote *yerd*, making nonsense of the line.
324. hele. The Roxb. ed. has *fele;* which is wrong.
325. chylde. This word seems to have crept in by mistake. The sense and alliteration would require 'blonk' = steed.
326. Thenne thei. The Roxb. ed. has *Thenne ether;* the transcriber having mistaken the last *e* in *then* for the beginning of the word *ether*.
staloworth. Miswritten for *stalworth*.
328. cheuelrye. *Sic* in MS.
330. benne = the time when.

331. *Ung serpent a deux testes,
oncques tel ne vit homme
. . . . saillit . . . . .
Tout droit a Mauquarre a sa veue
se lance
Les deux testes lui crevent les deux
yeulx sans doubtance.*
332. rapte, in MS.; *frapte*, which is a common word enough, would suit the alliteration better.
333. Thenne. *Sic* in MS. The Roxb. ed. has *whenne*.
334. '*Schreding*,' or some such word, is wanted instead of, or after, *Even*.
336. I shall þe ʒelde = I shall render unto thee = I shall serve thee, I shall requite thee.

¶ He trussethe his harneys fro þe nekke · & þe hede wynnethe;
Sythen he toke hit by þe lokkes · & in þe helm leyde;
Thoo thanked he our lorde lowely · þat lente hym þat grace.

Matabryne flees, but the child overtakes her and has her burnt to brown ashes.

Thenne sawe þe qwene matabryne · her man so murdered;   340
Turned her brydelle · & towarde þe towne rydethe;
The chylde folowethe here aftur · fersly & faste,
Sythen browȝte here aȝeyne · wo for to drye,
And brente here in þe balowe fyer · alle to browne askes.   344

The young Queen is unbound. Enyas tells his story to the King and Queen.

¶ The ȝonge qwene at þe fyre · by þat was vnbouñdeñ;
The childe kome byfore þe kynge · & on-hyȝe he seyde,
And tolde hym how he was his sone · '& oþur sex childereñ,
By þe qwene betryce · she bare hem at ones,   348
For a worde on þe walle · þat she wronge seyde;
And ȝonder in a ryuere · swymmen þey swañnes;
Sythen þe forsworne thefe Malkadras · byrafte hem her cheynes.'   351
'By god,' quod þe goldsmythe ·'I knowe þat ryȝth wele;

The goldsmith says he has five of the chains at home. They all go to the river and give the chains to the swans. Each choosing his own, turns to his human form. All but one. He, for want of his chain, remained always a swan.

¶ Fyve cheynes I haue · & þey ben fysh hole.'
Nowe withe þe goldsmyȝthe · gon alle þese knyȝtes,
Toke þey þe cheynes · & to þe watur turneñ,   355
And shoken vp þe cheynes · þer sterten vp þe swannes;
Eche on chese to his · & turneñ to her kynde:
But on was alwaye a swanne · for losse of his cheyne.
Hit was doole for to se · þe sorowe þat he made;
He bote hym self with his bylle · þat alle his breste bledde,   360

345. by þat = by that time.
353. fysh hole = 'as sound as a roach,' as we say.
356. shoken. *Sic* in MS. The former edition has *stroken*.
357. turneñ. The former edition has *turneden* in this place; but not in l. 355.
chese to his = chose his own.
358. alwaye. *Sic* in MS. Edition of 1820 has *always*.

THEY ARE CHRISTENED.   19

¶ And alle his feyre federes · fomede vpon blode,
And alle formerknes þe watur · þer þe swanne swym-
    methe :
There was ryche ne pore · þat myȝte for rewthe,   'Twas sad to see
Lengere loke on hym · but to þe courte wendeñ. 364   his sorrow.
Thenne þey formed a fonte · & cristene þe childreñ ; They christen the
And callen Vryens þat on · and Oryens another,   children.
Assakarye þe thrydde · & gadyfere þe fowrthe ;
The fyfte hette rose · for she was a maydeñ ;   368
The sixte was fulwedde · cheuelere assygne.
And þus þe botenynge of god · browȝte hem to honde.;. So by God's help
                                                       they were
                                                       restored.

.;. EXPLICIT .;.

362. formerknes. If this is *v. intr.*, and governed by the *sb.* water, it should have been by rights *formerkeneth* ; but if it is *pl.* and *tr.* governed by *federes*, it has borrowed the Northern *-es* termination instead of the Midland *-en*.

366. The names of the children in the French poem are *Orions, Orient, Zacharias, Jehan,* and *Rosette.*

369. was fulwedde = had been baptized already.

GLOSSARIAL INDEX.

ABBREVIATIONS.

Adj.	= Adjective.	*Obj.*	= Objective.
Adv.	= Adverb.	*O.E.*	= Old English, A.D. 500
Allit.	= Early Engl. Alliterative		—1200.
	Poems.	*Pf.*	= Perfect.
Art.	= Article.	*Pl.*	= Plural.
Comp.	= Comparative.	*P. pt.*	= Past Participle.
Conj.	= Conjunction.	*Pers.*	= Personal.
Cp.	= Compare.	*Poss.*	= Possessive.
Dem.	= Demonstrative.	*Prep.*	= Preposition.
Fem.	= Feminine.	*Pron.*	= Pronoun.
Fr.	= French.	*Refl.*	= Reflexive.
Gen.	= Genesis and Exodus.	*Rel.*	= Relative.
Germ.	= German.	*Sb.*	= Substantive.
Imp.	= Imperative.	*Sc.*	= Scottish.
Imp. pt.	= Imperfect Participle.	*Sing.*	= Singular.
Int.	= Interjection.	*Tr.*	= Transitive.
Intr.	= Intransitive.	*V.*	= Verb.

Wm. = William of Palerne.

A, *interj.* = Ah, 71, 82, 250, 255, 260.

A, *art.* 5, 6, &c. Perhaps as a numeral = one, 157, 165.

A, *prep.* = in, or on; O.E. & O. Sc. *An.* In l. 79 it means *at*.

Abbot, *sb.* 265.

Abowte, *prep.* 44, 126.

Abulle, *adj.* = fit, proper, able, 289.

Adowne, *adv.* = down, 21, 88, 101, 114; adown, 190, 297.

Affye, *sb.* = trust, 10.

Afore, *adv.* = in front, 228.

Aftur, *prep.* = along, 321; for, or in quest of, 46, 129, 153, 342; in accordance with, 13, 238; *adv.* = afterwards, 54, 80, 258, 271, 276; behind, 322.

Alle, *adj.* 43, 67, 98, &c.; *adv.* 15.

Alle-weldinge, *adj.* = Almighty, 1. O.E. *Eal-wealdende*.

Allewey. See Alwaye.

Allone, *adj.* = alone, 184.

Als, *conj.* = also, 91.
Also, *conj.* 218.
Alwaye, *adv.* 358; allewey, 305.
An, *art.* 5, 331, &c.
And, *conj.* 8, 18, &c. = an, if, 139.
Angelle, *sb.* 192, 193, 221.
Anon, *adv.* 85; anone, 68, 190, 258.
Another, *adj.* 268, 301, 366.
Ar, 3d *pl. pres. ind.* of *v.* Be, 82.
Armed, *p. pt.* of arm, *v. tr.* 283.
Armes, *sb. pl.* 262.
Armour, *sb.* 280.
Aryse, *v. intr.* 2d *sing. imper.* 77, 303.
As, *conj.* 7, 19, &c. = as though, 53.
Aske, *v. tr.* 128, 171; 3d *sing. pf.* askede, 130, 192; asskede, 210; *p. pt.* asked, 131.
Askes, *sb. pl.* = ashes, 344.
Asseylde, 3d *sing. pf. ind.* of asseyle, *v. tr.* 145.
Assygne = Fr. an cygne, 11, &c.
Assygyned, *p. pt.* of assign, *v. tr.* 188.
At, *prep.* 23, 60, 98.
Aw3te, *sb.* = aught, 204.
A3eyne, *adv.* = again, 93, 104, 137, 177, 343; a3eyn, 123.

Badde. *See* Bid.
Bakke, *sb.* = back, 291, 293.
Balowe, *adj.* O.E. *Bealu,* or *Bealo; Balo* or *Balu* = deadly, 233, 344, strong (?) 317.
Banke, *sb.* 132.
Barmeteme, *sb.* 103. This is the O.E. *Bearnteme,* and is miswritten for barnteme = brood, progeny, from barne = child, bairn; and teme, or teem (O.E. *teman*) = to produce, bring forth. *See* Ge 954 and 3903. In Chalmers's Li of James I. (prefixed to his 'Poet Remains of the Scottish king; 1824), p. 15, he writes, "The A of the former session was renewe in this; requiring the clergy pray for the king, for the quee and their *Bairntime,* which is no explained to mean, 'the childre produced between them.'"
Bathe, *v. tr.* 263.
Bare, 3d *sing. pf. ind.* of bear, *tr.* 325, 348.
Be, *v. intr.* 17, 37, 80; 3d *pl. pre subj.* bene (O.E. *beon*), 188; 3 *sing. subj.* 100, 302.
Bedde, *sb.* 33, 161.
Beetheth. *See* Bete.
Befalle, *v. intr.* 204.
Bene. *See* Be, *v. intr.*
Bere, *v. tr.* 3d *sing. ind.* beretl 297; 3d *sing. pf.* 196. *See al;* Bare, *p. pt.* borne, 23, 41.
Berthe. *See* Byrthe.
Beste, *sb.* = beast, 214; beeste 218, 288.
Beste, *adj.* 68, 285.
Bete, *v. tr.* O.E. *betan* = to pre pare, to kindle (said of fire); 3 *sing. pres. ind.* beetheth, 157; *j pt.* bette, 224.
Bete, *v. tr.* = beat; *imp. pt* betynge, 227.
Beteche, *v. tr. See* Bytake, 312
Bette. *See* Bete.
Better, *adj.* 49, 175; bettur *adv.* 97.
Betyde, *v. intr.* 103.
Betynge. *See* Bete.
Bid, *v. tr.* 3d *sing. pf.* badde 156, 172, 248, 263; 3d *sing. pres* byddyth, 262.
Bledde, 3d *sing. pf.* of bleed, *v intr.* 360.

GLOSSARIAL INDEX. 23

Blente, *p. pt.* of blind, *v. tr.* O.E. *blendian*, 325.

Blethely, *adv.* = blithely, cheerfully, 278.

Blode, *sb.* = blood, 361.

Blythe, *adj.* 154.

Body, *sb.* 244.

Book, *sb.* 7, 270.

Borne. *See* Bere, *v. tr.*

Bote, 3*d sing. pf.* of bite, *v. tr.* 360.

Botenning, *sb.* = remedy, succour, 370; from boten, *v. tr.* formed from bote = remedy, from O.E. *gebetan* = to mend.

Bothe, *conj.* 20, 79 ; *adj.* 135.

Bounden, *p. pt.* of bind, *v. tr.* 291.

Boy, *sb.* 260 ; *poss.* boyes, 263.

Bowethe, 3*d sing. pres. ind.* of bow, *v. tr.* 335 ; bowethe hym, 265 = turneth him, goeth.

Breke, *v. tr.* O.E. *brecan;* 3*d sing. pres.* brekethe, 157 ; 1*st sing. pf. ind.* breke (now brake, or broke), 165.

Brenne, *v. tr.* = burn, 68, 241 ; *pf.* brente, 344; *p. pt.* brente, 80; intransitively, 191, 224.

Breste, *sb.* 297, 360 ; *pl.* brestes, 241.

Breste, *v. inter.* = burst, 317.

Broode, *adj.* = broad, 297.

Browne, *adj.* 344.

Broȝte, 3*d sing. pf.* of bring, *v. tr.* 41, 49, 343, 370.

Brydelle, *sb.* 229, 292, 341.

Brynge, *v. tr.* 2*d sing. imp.* 203.

Bryȝt, *adj.* = bright, 8 ; bryȝte, 298.

Busk, *v. tr.* = prepare, make ready ; 3*d sing. pf. ind.* buskede, 172; *p. pt.* buskedde, 233.

But, *conj.* 15, 17, &c. = except, 38 ; only, 242.

By, *prep.* 196, 348 ; = of, concerning, 5 ; at, about, 84, 143, 205 ; through, 85, 216, *adv.* = near, 109.

Bycche, *sb.* = bitch, 62.

Bydeste = abidest, 256, 2*d sing. ind.* of byde, *v. intr.*

Byddynge, *sb.* = command, 85.

Byddyth. *See* Bid.

Byfore, *prep.* = before, 23, 64, 110, 124, &c., before, 114.

Byforne, *adv.* = before, 322 (Wm. *biforn.* Gen. *biforen*).

Bygyleth, *p. pt.* of beguile, *v. tr.* (for beguiled), 78.

Byginne, *v. tr.* 3*d sing. pres. ina.* bygynnethe, 76, 246 ; 3*d sing. pf.* byganne, 183.

Byhelde, 3*d sing. pf.* of byhold = behold, 21.

Bylefte, *p. pt.* of byleve, or beleave = abandon, 240.

Bylle, *sb.* = bill, 360.

Byrafte, 3*d sing. pf. ind.* of byreave *or* bereave. O.E. *bereafian;* 199, 351.

Byrthe, *sb.* = birth, 23, 40, 291 ; berthe, 65.

Byside, *adv.* = beside, 149.

Bytake (*or* bitake) = betake, commit, deliver. O.E. *betæcan;* 3*d sing. pres. ind.* bytakethe, 151 ; bytaketh, 173 ; *p. pt.* bytaken, 163; cp. Gen. 212.

Call, *v. tr.* 3*d pl. pres. indic.* callen, 366 ; kallen, 292, 296 ; 3*d pl. pf.* called, 46 ; kallede, 270 ; 2*d sing. imp.* kalle, 204 ; *p. pt.* called, 289 ; kalled, 6, 231.

Caste, *v. tr.* 52 ; 3*d pl. pres. ind.* caste, 88 ; 1*st sing. pf.* caste, 167 ; 3*d sing.* caste, 63.

Cawsed, 3*d sing. pf. ind.* of cause, *v. tr.* 39

Certeyne, *adj.* = certain, 253.
Charde, *v. intr.* = care, 329.
Charge, *sb.* concern, 235.
Chaste, *sb.* = chest, 127. *See* Note.
Chaunce, *sb.* 123.
Chefe, *sb.* = chief, 11.
Cherye, *sb.* = cherry, 329.
Chese, 3d *sing. pf.* of choose. Used with the *prep.* to, 357.
Cheualere, *sb.* 11, 333; cheuelere, 369.
Cheuelrye, *sb.* miswritten for cheuelere, 328.
Cheuene, *v. tr.* quasi chiefen = to rule over, 16.
Cheuerynge, *imp. pt.* of cheuer or chyuer, q. v.
Cheyne, *sb.* 43, 125, 137, 146, 148, 150, 157, 164, 165, 176, 179, 199, 351.
Choppe, *v. tr.* 330.
Chylde, *sb.* = child, 16, 29, &c. With chylde, 35; *pl.* chylderen, 23, 82, 93; chyldren, 107, 122, 130, &c.; children, 143; childeren, 347.
Chyuer, *v. intr.* = shiver, 3d *pl. pf.* chyuered, 107; *imp. pt.* cheuerynge, 107. Cp. Morte Arthur (Linc.) l. 3392.
Clene, *adj.* 174.
Clensen, *v. tr.* = to cleanse, 247.
Close, *sb.* = an enclosed field, or space of ground, 272.
Clothe, *sb.* = cloth, 97.
Colde, *sb.* 107.
Combred (*p. pt.* of combre (cumber) = to trouble) = miserable, 71.
Come, *v. intr.* 38; com, 248; 2d *sing. pres. indic.* comeste, 51; 3d *sing.* comethe, 109; *pf.* come, 64, 110, 142, 151, 173, 183, 208, 228, 248; Kome, 113, 346; *p. pt.* comen, 154.

Confounde, *v. tr.* 75.
Countes, *sb.* = countess, 269.
Counselle, *sb.* 50.
Courte, *sb.* 53, 123, 163, 203; cowrte, 150, 155, &c.
Cowche, *sb.* = bed, 45.
Cowpe, *sb.* = cup, 153, 164, 173, &c.
Crafte, *sb.* = business, 313.
Criste, 104; Cryste, 111.
Cristen, *v. tr.* = christen, 266; 3d *pl. pres. ind.* cristene, 365; *p. pt.* cristened, 203, 275.
Crosse, *sb.* 281.
Crowne, *sb.* 237.
Croyse, *sb.* = cross, 328-9; croys, 332.
Cry, *v. intr.* 3d *sing. pres. ind.* cryethe, 81; 3d *pl. pf.* cryedde, 106; cryde, 108; cryede, 111.
Cuppe, *sb.* 160, 168.
Cursed, *p. pt.* of curse, *v. tr.* 38, 145; used adjectively, cursede, 142; cursedde, 121.
Curteynesse, *sb.* = courteousness, 179.

Dame, *sb.* 69, 73, 125, 132, 250.
Damme, *sb.* = mother, 61.
Dare, *v. intr.* 1st *sing. pres. ind.* 27; 3d *sing. pf.* durste, 56; *pl.* 147.
Day, *sb.* 188, 191, 208.
Dedde. *See* Done.
Dede, *sb.* = deed, 274.
Deepe, *adv.* 86.
Delyuered, *p. pt.* of delyuer, *v. tr.* 37, 180; 3d *sing. pf.* 155, 178.
Deseruethe, 3d *sing. pres.* of deserve, *v. tr.* 72.
Deth, *sb.* 100; dethe, 138, 182, 186.
Do, *v. tr.* 139; done, 238; 3d *sing. pf.* 172; 2d *sing. imper.* do, 138 *p. pt.* don, 235.

GLOSSARIAL INDEX. 25

Dole, *sb.* = sorrow, compassion, 134; doole, 359.
Dolefulle, *adj.* 106.
Dome, *sb.* = doom, 186; *pl.* domus, 91.
Dore, *sb.* 60, 87.
Down, *adv.* 305, 334, 335.
Dowȝter, *sb.* = daughter, 42.
Draw, *v. tr.* O.E. *dragan* (intransitively used, as in the phrase 'Draw near'); 3d *sing.* and *pl.* drowȝ, 33; and drowȝe, 37, 114, 161.
Drowȝe = drew (Gen. 1. 2360, dragen. O.E. *drog*). *See* Draw.
Drye, *v. tr.* (O.E. *dreogan.* Gen. *dregen*; Allit. *dryȝe*) = to dree, to suffer, 343.
Dryue, *v. tr.* dryue out = bring out, ascertain, 259.
Dubbede, 3d *sing. pf. ind.* 276.
Durste. *See* Dare.
Dwellest, 2d *sing. pres. ind.* of dwell, *v. intr.* 201; 3d *sing. pf.* dwellede, 13.
Dymme, *adj.* = dim, dark, 86.
Dynte, *sb.* 138.

Eche, *adj.* = each, 31, 44, 126; each a, O.E. *ilka* = each, every, 187.
Edder, *sb.* = adder, 331.
Eggelynges, *adv.* = edgelings, edgewise, with the edge (O.E. *Ecg.* = edge), 305.
Eke, *adv.* = also, 180.
Elles, *adv.* = else (Allit. *elleȝ*), 74, 215, 290; ellis, 30.
Elleven, *adj.* 89.
Ende, *sb.* 40, 240; *v. tr.* 330.
Enforme, *v. tr.* 212.
Er, *prep.* = ere, before, 70.
Erle, *sb.* 268.
Erthe, *sb.* 320.

Etethe, 3d *sing. pres. ind.* of ete (eat), 290.
Euen, 243, 334.
Euur = ever, 222, 322.
Eyther = each, 220, 318, 320.

Fader, *sb.* = father, 90, 212, 219; *poss.* fader, 203.
Fallethe, *p. pt.* of fall = falled, 310. Perhaps miswritten for *felled*; which is the more likely, as the *p. pt.* of *fall* ought to be *fallen*; while *fell* would make *felled*. We say, however, sometimes, ' To *fall* timber.'
False, *adj.* 257; fals, 239.
Faste, *adv.* 141, 223, 227, 304, 309, 342.
Fastened, *p. pt.* of fasten, *v. tr.* 319.
Fayre, *adj.* 90; feyre, 217, 266, 275, 361.
Febull, *adj.* = sad, bad, 58; used *substantively*, 76.
Feder, *sb.* = feather; *pl.* federes, 361.
Felawe, *sb.* = fellow, 258.
Felde, *sb.* = field, 223, 319.
Felle, *adj.* = severe, stern, cruel, 239.
Felle, *pf.* of fall, *v. intr.* 110, 114; 3d *pl.* 148; = befell, 130.
Felly, *adv.* = sternly, cruelly, fiercely, 76, 225. The word is used by Spenser.
Fende, *sb.* = fiend, devil, 120; fend, 240.
Fere, *sb.* = companion, 325.
Fersly, *adv.* = fiercely, 342.
Ferther, *adv.* (*comp.*) = further, 127.
Fete, *sb.* (*pl.* of foot) 303, 323.
Fette, *p. pt.* of fette, *v. tr.* = fetch, 279.

Feyth, *sb.* 48; feythe, 121, 130, 142.

Find, *v. ir. p. pt.* fownden, 239; 2*d sing. indic.* fyndes, 305.

Flesh, *sb.* 310.

Fleye, 3*d pl. pf.* of fly, *v. intr.* 319.

Flowen, 3*d pl. pf.* of the same, 148 (Allit. *flowen*; Gen. *flogen*).

Folke, *sb.* 187, 223.

Folowe, *v. tr.* 2*d sing. imper.* 310; 3*d sing. pres. ind.* foloweth, 116, 342.

Fomede, 3*d pl. pf. ind.* of fome (foam), *v. intr.* 361.

Fonte, *sb.* 267, 365.

For, *conj.* 3, 5, &c.; *prep.* 15, 29, 49, &c.

Foreste, *sb.* 95.

Forge, *v. tr.* 153.

Forlonge, *sb.* = furlong, 228.

Formed, 3*d pl. pf.* of form, *v. tr.* 365; *p. pt.* formeth = formed, 200, 209.

Formerken, *v. intr.* = darken; 3*d sing. indic.* formerknes, 362. *See* Note.

Forsette, *v. tr.* = beset, entrap, betray, 251. O.E. *forsettan.* Cp. Allit. B. 78.

Forsothe, *adv.* 18, 195, 242.

Forsworn, *p. pt.* of forswear, *v. tr.* 199; forsworne, 351.

Forthe, *adv.* 52, 60, 75, &c. Forth, 176.

Forthy, *adv.* = wherefore, 218 (O.E.).

Fostere, *sb.* = forester, 120.

Fowle, *adj.* 40, 239.

Fownden. *See* Find.

Fowre, *numeral adj.* = four, 95.

Fowrth, *adj.* = fourth, 367.

Frapte, *pf.* of frap = strike, 332.

Frely, *adj.* = lordly, noble, 218,
266, 275. Cp. Allit. B. 162; Wm. 124.

Freshe, *adj.* 258.

Fro, *prep.* 113, 148, 159, 298, 328.

Frusch, *v. intr.* (properly *tr.* = strike. Fr. *froisser*) but here = rush; 3*d sing. ind.* fruscheth, 332.

Fulfylde, *p. pt.* of fulfylle (fulfil), 206.

Fulle, *adv.* 12, 54, 69, 113, 141, &c.

Fulwen, *v. tr.* = baptize. O.E. *fulwian*; *p. pt.* fulwedde, 369.

Furre, *comp.* of fur = further, 311.

Fyfte, *adj.* = fifth, 368.

Fyndes. *See* Find, *v. tr.*

Fyre, *sb.* 224, 233, 332, 345; fyer, 159, 165, 167, 344.

Fyrste, *adj.* 51, 58; *adv.* 80.

Fysh, *sb.* = fish, 353.

Fyue, *numeral adj.* 159; fyve, 167.

Fyʒte, *v. intr.* = fight, 200, 209, 212, 245, 259; *sb.* 273.

Gader, *v. intr.* = gather; *imp. pt.* gaderynge, 223.

Gete, *v. tr.* = get, 261; 3*d sing. pf. ind.* gette (properly ʒet or ʒat), 34; 2*d sing. imper.* gete, 137.

Gladdenes, *sb.* 57.

Go, *v. intr.* 3*d sing. pres. ind.* goothe, 157; 3*d pl.* gon, 354; *p. pt.* go, 143.

God, *sb.* 1, 40, &c.; *poss.* goddes, 206, 219.

Godfader, *sb.* 267.

Godmoder, *sb.* 269.

Goldsmyʒte, *sb.* 153, 157, 354; goldsmythe, 352.

Good, *adj.* 130, 289.

Grace, *sb.* 302, 339.

GLOSSARIAL INDEX. 27

Graunt, *v. tr.* = grant ; 2*d sing. pf. ind.* grauntethe, 278 ; 3*d sing.* graunted, 189, 246.

Grete, *adj.* = great, 83 ; gret, 264.

Grownde, *sb.* 302.

Grymme, *adj.* black, dark, 51 ; sad, 189. Cp. Allit. A. 1069.

Grypte, 3*d sing. pf.* of gryp, *v. tr.* 220.

Gynnyth, 3*d sing. pres. ind.* of gynne, *v.* (begin), 66.

Hadde. *See* Haue.

Halen, *v. tr.* = to haul ; 3*d pl. indic.* halenne, 280.

Halfe, *sb.* 165 ; = side, behalf, 219.

Haluendele = half-deal = half, 176 ; halvendelle, 160.

Ham, *pers. pron. obj.* = them, 152.

Happe, *sb.* = hap (good), 324.

Harm, *sb.* 235 ; harme, 3.

Harnes, *sb.* = armour, 278 ; harneys, 337.

Hast. *See* Haue.

Hatefulle, *adj.* 141.

Hath. *See* Haue.

Haue, *v. tr.* 120 ; 1*st sing. pres. ind.* 70, 353 ; 2*d sing.* hast, 78 ; haste, 194, 251, 310 ; 3*d sing.* hath, 128 ; 3*d pl.* haue, 79 ; 3*d sing. pf.* hadde, 16, 44, 47 ; 1*st sing. pf. subj.* 181 ; 2*d sing.* 53 ; *p. pt.* hadde, 79.

Hawberke, *sb.* 296.

He, *pers. pron.* 2, 13, &c.

Hedde, *sb.* = head, 27, 217, 257 ; hede, 295 ; heede, 311.

Heelde. *See* Holden, *v. tr.*

Heete (*or* Hete), *v. tr.* = tell ; 1*st sing. pres. indic.* 18.

Hele, *sb.* = pleasure, advantage, 324. O.E. *Hel* = health.

Helle, *sb.* 10.

Helme = helmet, *sb.* 296, 306, 338.

Helpe, *sb.* 118, 247, 273.

Helpe, *v. tr.* 50 ; 3*d sing. pres. subj.* 70.

Hem, *pron.* = 'em, them ; 19, 20, 44, 45, 52, 83, 96, 97, 101, 102, 104, 109, 110, 112, 114—119, 126, 129, 133, 134, 138, 148, 151, 152, 159, 169, 190, 194, 196, 199, 316, 318—320, 348, 351.

Hemselfen = themselves, 20.

Hente, *v. tr.* = seize, take ; 3*d pl. pf. ind.* hente, 85 ; *p. pt.* hente, 3.

Her, *poss. pron. fem.* 10, 32, 340, 341.

Her, *pers. pron. fem. obj.* 23, 35, 38, 47, 68, 70, 73, 85, 176, 262.

Her, *adv.* = here, in this place, 77.

Her = their. *See* Here.

Here, *poss. pron. fem.* = her, 171, 182, 240, 255.

Here, *pers. pron. fem. obj.* = her, 15, 32, 34, 86—88, 126, 131, 135, 151, 153, 189, 190, 226, 342—344.

Here, *poss. pron. pl.* = their, 126, 220, 235, 274, 315, 321 ; her, 105, 199, 327.

Here, *v. tr.* = hear, 57 ; 1*st sing. pf. ind.* herde, 213 ; 3*d sing.* 55, 58, 108 ; 2*d sing. imper.* 131.

Here, *sb.* = hair ; *pl.* heres, 255.

Heremyte, *sb.* 115, 221 ; hermyte, 109, 192, 201.

Herseluen = herself, 47.

Herte, *sb.* (Germ. *herz*) = heart, 18, 189, 263, 334.

Hette, 3*d sing. pres. indic.* = is called, 232 ; 3*d sing. pf.* hette, 7 ; hyȝte, 9. (O.E. *hatan* = to be called.)

His, *poss. pron. masc.* 2, 8, 36, &c. ; hys, 135.

Hit, *pers. pron. neut.* 30, 72, 74, &c.

Holden, *v. tr.* = to hold, 169; 3*d sing. pf. ind.* heelde, 152; 2*d sing. imper.* holde, 127; *p. pt.* holde = accounted, 70.

Hole, *sb.* 294.

Hole, *adj.* = whole, 353.

Hollye, *adv.* = wholly, 160, 168, 181.

Holy, *adj.* 109, 265.

Honde, *sb.* = hand, 2, 41, 152, 158, 164, 166, 174, 220, 255, 287, 300, 315, 370.

Hondredde = hundred, 255.

Honged, 3*d sing. pf.* of hongen, or hangen = hang, 18.

Hors, *sb.* = horse, 213, 289; *pl.* horses, 321.

Houe, *v. intr.* = to abide still, to hover, to wait, 288. Cp. Allit. B. 927; and Lancelot, 996.

How, *adv.* 26, 31, &c.

Hownde, *sb. pl.* howndes, 79, 234.

Hy, *adj.* = high, 326; hye, 217; hyȝ, 224; hyȝe, 280; on hyȝe = aloud.

Hylyde, 3*d sing. pf.* of hylen = hele = cover, 102.

Hym, *pers. pron. masc. obj.* = him, 4, 24, &c.

Hym *for* Hem = them, 52.

Hynde, *sb.* 113, 116.

Hytte, *v. tr.* 300.

Hyȝe, *adj.* See Hy.

Hyȝe, *v. intr.* = hie, go, 139; *refl.* 3*d sing. pf.* hyed hym, 141.

Hyȝnes, *sb.* = highness, 4.

Hyȝte = was called. *See* Hette.

I, *pers. pron.* 5, 18, &c.

If, *conj.* 192.

In, *prep.* 4, 5, &c.

Is, 3*d sing. pres. ind.* of Be, *v. intr.* 1, 26, &c.

It, *pers. pron. neut.* 1, 12, &c.

Joye, *sb.* 246.

Juge = judge, 236. *See* Note.

Kalled, &c. *See* Call.

Kan, *v. tr.* = can, i. e. know; 1*st sing. pres. ind.* kan, 311, 313; 2*d sing.* kanste, 212; 1*st sing. pf.* kowthe = knew, 313.

Kawȝte, 3*d sing. pf. ind.* of catch, 287; in l. 62 it = snatched Cp. 'caught up.'

Keene, *adj.* 183; used *adverbially*.

Kenely, *adv.* 309.

Kepe, *v. tr.* = keep, 50^s; 3*d sing. pf. ind.* kepte, 117, 174; 2*d sing. imper.* kepe, 328.

Keste, 3*d sing. pf. indic.* of cast, 97.

Knee, *sb. pl.* knees, 110.

Knowe, *v. tr.* 97; 1*st sing. pres. ind.* 309, 352; 2*d sing.* knoweste, 251; 3*d sing. pf.* knewe, 49.

Knyfe, *sb.* 62.

Knyȝte, *sb.* = knight, 258, 276, 287, 289; *pl.* knyȝtes, 354.

Kome. *See* Come.

Kowarde, *sb.* 71.

Kowth. *See* Kan.

Kylled, 3*d sing. pf.* of kylle (kill); *v. tr.* 62.

Kynde, *sb.* (kind) = nature, condition, 71, 276; kin, family. 11. Cp. Gen. 650.

Kynge, *sb.* 7, 20, &c.; *poss.* kynges, 195.

Kyrtelle, *sb.* 294.

Ladde. *See* Lead, *v. tr.* Spenser uses this inflection, F. Q., I. i. 4 'a milke white lamb she *lad*.'

Lady, *sb.* 82, 89, 92, 191.

Lafte. *See* Leve, *v. tr.*

Langour, *sb.* = languor, 15, 57, 92.

Lappe, *sb.* 257.

Lappe, *v. tr.* = wrap ; 3*d sing. pf.* lappede, 102 ; *p. pt.* lapped, 132 ; lappedde, 101.

Lassche, *v. tr.* = strike (lash out = kick); 3*d sing pres. ind.* lasscheth, 323.

Laste, *adj.* 240.

Launce, *sb.* 300.

Launce, *v. tr.* = launce, dart, throw ; 3*d sing. pres. ind.* launces, 323.

Laye. See Lye, *v. intr.*

Lead, *v. tr.* 3*d sing. pf. ind.* ladde, 287.

Lefe, *adj.* = dear, 82.

Lefte, *pf.* of leve, q. v.

Lefte, 3*d sing. pf. ind.* of lift (O.E. *Lefan*), 45.

Lende, *v. intr.* a form of leng = tarry, abide ; *p. pt.* lente, 'was lente,' l. 5 = dwelt. Cp. Allit. B. 1084, 'waʒt lent.'

Lendeth, 3*d sing. pres. ind.* of lend, *v. tr.* 99.

Lene, *v. tr.* = lend, grant, 277, 284 ; *p. pt.* lente, 112, 339.

Leng, *v. intr.* = tarry, dwell ; 3*d sing. pres. ind.* lengeth, 4.

Lengur, *adv., comp.* of long, 77, 112, 303 ; lengere, 364.

Lente. See Lende, *v. intr.* ; and Lene, *v. tr.*

Lepte, 3*d sing. pf. ind.* of lepe (leap), *v. intr.* 254.

Let, *v. tr.* = allow, cause ; 3*d sing. pf. ind.* lette, 24, 190 ; 2*d sing. imper.* lette, 187 ; lete, 307 ; 2*d sing. subj.* lete, 52.

Leue, *v. tr.* = believe, allow, 28, 133 ; leeue, 242.

Leue, *v. tr.* = leave ; 1*st sing. pf. ind.* lafte, 133 ; 3*d sing.* 17, 221 ; 1*st pl. imper.* leue, 92 ; 3*d pl. pres. ind.* leuen, 87. Also *intransitively* = remain ; 3*d sing. pf. ind.* lefte, 175 ; leued, 255.

Leues, *sb. pl.* of lefe (leaf), 119.

Ley. See Lye, *v. intr.*

Leyde, 1*st sing. pf. ind.* of lay ; *v. tr.* 165 ; 3*d sing.* 87, 101, 159, 338.

Leyne, *v. tr.* = grant, requite, reward, 99.

Lofe, *sb.* = love, 15.

Loke, *v. intr.* = look, 364 ; 3*d sing. pf. ind.* loked, 21 ; 3*d sing. imper.* looke, 52 ; loke, 203, 300.

Lokke, *sb.* of a door, 87 ; of hair, 254; *pl.* lokkes, 338.

Londe, *sb.* = land, 6, 181, 231 ; *pl.* londis, 16.

Longe, *adj.* 95, 299 ; *adv.* 47, 185.

Lorde, *sb.* 5, 36, 70, &c.

Lordeles, *adj.* = having no lord, or sovereign, 17.

Losse, *sb.* 358.

Lothe, *adj.* 249 ; loth, 48.

Loue, *sb.* 36.

Loue, *v. tr.* 14.

Louely, *adv.* 98.

Lowde, *adj.* 225.

Lowely, *adv.* = meekly, humbly, 36, 339.

Lowʒe, 3*d pl. pf. indic.* of laʒe, *v. intr.* = laugh, 98.

Lye, *v. intr.* 257 ; 3*d sing. pf. ind.* lay, 57, 207 ; laye, 76 ; 3*d pl.* ley, 98 ; *imp. pt.* lyyinge, 133.

Lyf, *sb.* = life, 17 ; lyfe, 112, 335.

Lyfe, *v. intr.* = live, 54.

Lyfte, *v. tr.* 299.

Lyke, *v.* = like, 54 (*see* Note), 140 ; 3*d sing. pres. ind.* lykes, 134 ; lyketh, 73.

Lykynge, *sb.* = liking, 13.

Lyme, *sb.* = limb ; *pl.* lymes, 217.

Lyonys, *pl.* of lyon ; *sb.* 214.

Lytulle, *adj.* 242.
Lyue, *v. intr.* = live ; 3*d sing. pf. ind.* lyuede, 89.
Lyue, *sb.* = life, 140.
Lyuinge, *adj.* = living, 256.
Lyʒtly, *adv.* = lightly, 303.

Made. } *See* Make.
Maden. }

Make, *v. tr.* 3*d sing. pres. ind.* maketh, 267 ; 3*d sing. pf.* made, 9, 83, 90, 135, 359 ; 3*d pl.* maden, 314.

Man, *sb.* 46, 108, &c. ; manne, 29 ; *poss.* mannes, 273 ; *pl.* men, 79, 94 ; menne, 285.

Mantelle, *sb.* 101, 105, 132.
Many, *adj.* 31, 34, &c.
Marre, *sb.* = mar, *v. tr.* 261.
Mater, *sb.* = matter, 216.
May, 1*st sing. pres. ind.* of mowe = to be able = can, 74, 295 ; 2*d sing.* 50, 54 ; also mayste, 249.
Mayden, *sb.* 368.
Me, *indeterm. pron.* (Germ. *man* ; Fr. *on*) 30.
Me, *pers. pron. obj.* 70, 261.
Mene, *v. tr.* mention ; 3*d sing. pf. ind.* menede, 124.
Mengynge, *sb.* = mingling, twisting, 125. From menge, *v. tr.* = mix.
Meruelows, *adj.* (used *adverbially*) 185.
Merueyle, *sb.* 125.
Mesure, *sb.* 171.
Mete, *sb.* = meat, 88, 144.
Moche, *adj.* = much, 9, 39, 102, 136 ; *substantively*, 184.
Moder, *sb.* = mother, 9, 39, 59, 180, 200, 205, 209, 210.
Mone, *sb.* = moan, 83, 136.
Mony, *adj.* 90, 124, 271.

More, *adj.* 88, 125, 171.
Morn, *sb.* = morning, 183.
Morne, *v. intr.* = mourn, 66.
Morwe, *sb.* = morrow, 172.
Most, *v.* = must, 2*d sing. in*(of mot, 50, 206 ; 3*d sing.* 136, 20(
See Mote.
Moste, *adv.* 285.
Mote, 3*d sing. pres. subj.* (mot, 120. The word has in th phrase an optative force. *See* Mos
Mowthe, *sb.* = mouth, 292.
Multiplyeth, 3*d sing. pres. in*(of multiply ; *v. intr.* 158.
Murdered, *p. pt.* of murder, *tr.* 340.
Murther, *v. tr.* 94, 129.
My, *poss. pron.* 27, 78, 82, 10(&c
Mydday, *sb.* 205.
Myle, *sb.* 95.
Myne, *poss. pron.* 181.
Mysfare, *v. intr.* = go wrong, 23ʇ
Myskarye, *v. intr.* = miscarr) 260.
Myssede, 3*d sing. pf. ind.* (mysse (miss), *v. tr.* 83.
Myʒte = might, 1*st sing. pf. in*(of mowe, or mowen, *v.* 134 ; 3 *sing.* 14, 247, 363 ; 1*st pl.* 3.

Name, *sb.* 204, 270.
Nay, *interj.* 28.
Ne = not, 3, 147.
Nekke, *sb.* 297, 337.
Nere, *prep.* = near, 38.
Nere, *v.* = ne were, 4.
Neuur, *adv.* = never, 202, 216.
Neythur, *adv.* 253 ; *sb.* 306.
No, *adj.* 16, 38, 77.
None = ne one, 127, 216 : *adj* 250.

Noryscheth, 3d sing. pres. ind. of norysch (nourish); v. tr. 118.
Not, adv. 28.
Nother, conj. = nor, 253.
Nowe, adv. 354.
Now3te, sb. = nought, 53.
Noyse, sb. 225.
No3t, adv. = not, 236, 295; no3te, 74.
No3the, sb. = nought, 290; now3te, 53.
Nykke, v. tr. = refuse, contradict; = ne (not), ikke (say); cognate with Latin *Negare*. With *ikke* compare Gothic *Aikan*; Sanskrit *Ah* = to say, to speak; Latin *Ajo* (agjo). Cp. also the Sanskrit *Aham* = I, with the O.E. *Ic*.
Ny3e, adj. = nigh, 100.
Ny3te, sb. = night, 33, 34, 161, 191.

Of, prep. 4, 10, &c. = from, out of, 287; = adv. off, 146, 311.
Ofte, adv. 3, 111.
Olde, adj. 163, 227, 243, &c.
On, prep. 34, 207.
On, num. = one, 44, 126, 143, 249, 295, 297, 299, 357, 358; oon, 29, 285.
One, num. 264.
One, adj. = alone, 15, 19.
Ones, adv. = at ones = at once, 98, 196, 272, 348.
On-hy3e, adv. = aloud, 25, 64, 106, 234, 346; on hy3, 81; on-hy = up, 326.
Ony, adj. = any, 175, 273.
Oo-lyuynge, adj. = everliving, eternal, 201.
Oon. See On.
Orysoun, sb. = prayer, 90.
Other, adj. 144, 145, 296, &c.; othur, 159, 167, 347.

Other, conj. = or (Germ. *oder*), 324.
Our, poss. pron. 36, 70, 93, 117.
Out, for drew, or pulled out, 146.
Ouur, adv. = over, 175.
Owne, 2, 14, &c.

Pappe, sb. = breast, 114.
Paye, v. tr. = please, 65.
Peces, pl. of pece (piece), 315.
Pele, v. intr. smite, 'let drive,' 304. Cp. peal (of bells), sb.; also pelt, v. Mr Skeat writes, "Perhaps this is an instance of the word *Pelle*, which occurs in Havelok, and *nowhere else*, unless it is *here*. In Havelok it = drive forth, go; and seems to be the Lat. *pellere*.
The line in Havelok is,
'Shal ich neuere lenger dwelle,
To morwen shall ich forth *pelle*.'
                    ll. 809-10.
[' I shall stay here no longer,
I shall start off to-morrow!
It answers to our expression, 'go full drive.'"
Place, sb. 12.
Plesed, p. pt. of plese (please); v. tr. 274.
Plukke, v. tr. 2d sing. imper. 304.
Pore, adj. = poor, 22, 26, 363.
Posse, sb. Perhaps miswritten for Poste, 281.
Prayde, 3d sing. pf. ind. of pray; v. tr. 284; 2d sing. pres. prayeth, 277.
Preste, adj. = ready, 135.
Prestly, adv. = readily, quickly, 277.
Preve, v. tr. = prove, 252.
Price, adj. = worthy, noble, 279. Comp. Wm. l. 411.
Prisoun, sb. 80; prysoun, 86.

GLOSSARIAL INDEX.

Prowde, *adj.* 115.

Pulledde, 3*d pl. pf.* of pulle ; *v. tr.* 327.

Putte, *v. tr.*, 3*d sing. pf. ind.* putte, 115 ; putt, 135.

Pyne, *sb.* = suffering, 92. O.E. *pin* ; *v. tr.* = to make to suffer, to torment, 26. O.E. *pinan*.

Pytte, *sb.* = pit, 63.

Quod *or* quoth, 3*d sing. pf. ind.* = said, 71, 99, 169, 214—216, 219, 230, 236, 242, 250, 256, 260, 288, 289, 290, 312, 328-29, 336, 352. O.E. *cwæð*, of *Cweðan* = to say.

Qwene, *sb.* = queen, 8, 14, &c.

Raunges, *sb. pl.* = lists, 314, 321. Cp. 'ringes' in Sir Eglamore, l. 1121, Percy folio, p. 382, vol. 2.

Raw3te (Raught). *See* Reche.

Reasonabullye, *adv.* = reasonably, 34.

Rebukede, 3*d sing. pf.* of rebuke, 32.

Reche, *v. tr.* = reach ; 3*d sing. pres. ind.* recheth, 176 ; 3*d pl. pf.* raw3ten, 316.

Recke, *v. intr.* = reck, care ; 3*d sing. pf. ind.* row3te, 177 ; 2*d sing. imper.* rekke, 306.

Rede, *v. tr.* = advise, 222 ; 1*st sing. pres. ind.* rede, 169.

Redresse, *v. tr.* 205.

Rekke. *See* Recke.

Rennen, *v. intr.* = run, 316 (?); *imp. pt.* rennynge, 113 ; 3*d pl. pf.* ronnen, 314, 321. *Rennene*, 316, may be *sb.* = rennenge *or* running, but is more likely the verb above.

Reredde, *p. pt.* of rere (rear) ; *v. tr.* 211.

Reste, *v. tr.* 77 ; 2*d sing. imper.* reste, 303.

Rewede, 3*d sing. pf. ind.* of rewe (rue) ; *v. tr.* = repent, be sorry for ; used *impersonally*, 55 ; hym rewede = he was sorry.

Rewfulle, *adj.* 149.

Rewthe, *sb.* = ruth, sorrow, 102, 363.

Ring, *v. intr.*, 3*d pl. pf. ind.* rongen, 272.

Rongen. *See* Ring.

Rowte, *sb.* = crowd, 287.

Row3te. *See* Rekke, *v. intr.*

Ryche, *adj.* 271, 306, 363.

Rydethe, 3*d sing. pres. ind.* of ryde (ride); *v. intr.* 341 ; rydinge, *p. pt.* 228.

Ryuer, *sb.* 198 ; ryuere, 149, 350 ; *poss.* ryueres, 132.

Ry3te, *adj.* = right, 222, 236, 336, 352 ; *sb.* 259 ; *pl.* 'his ry3tes,' 283 ; *adv.* 32, 198, 205, 249.

Ry3[t]lye, *adv.* = rightly, 236.

Sadde, *adj.* 119. Perhaps = solid, massive (Cp. Wm. 1072) ; or else, and more probably = shed (O.E. *scaden*, from *scadan, v. tr.* Germ. *scheiden*). Cp. Gen. l. 58.

Sadelle, *sb.* 293.

Safe, *adj.* 43.

Same, *adj.* 34.

Saue, *v. tr.* 91 ; 3*d sing. pf. ind.* saued, 91.

Sauinge, *sb.* 194.

Sawe, *sb.* = that which is said, tale, 162, 253. *See also* Se, *v. tr.*

Sayde. *See* Seye.

Saye. *See* Se, *v. tr.*

Scharpelye, *adv.* 301.

Schreden, *v. tr.* = shred, 307.

Schyuered. *See* Shyuer.

Se, *v. tr.* = see, 359 ; 3*d sing. pres. ind.* seeth, 223 ; 1*st sing. pf.* saye, 5 ; sey3e, 216 ; 3*d sing.* sey3, 22 ; sy3e, 202 ; sawe, 61 340 ; 3*d sing. imper.* se, 26 ; used with *prep.*

GLOSSARIAL INDEX. 33

of, 65; *1st sing. pres. subj.* 74; *p. pt.* sene, 53.

Seche, *v. tr.* = seek; *2d sing. imper.* seche, 53; *3d sing. pf. ind.* sowȝte, 60. Used intransitively in both places, in the sense of To betake oneself, go.

Seke, *v. tr.* = seek, 144.

Selfe, 73.

Selfen *or* Selven = self, and selves, 20, 47.

Seluer = silver, 43; seluere, 125.

Semelye, *adj.* = seemly, 42.

Sende, *v. tr.* 111; *3d sing. pres. ind.* sendethe, 88, 118; sendeth, 193; *3d sing. pf.* sente, 46, 129, 153.

Serue, *v. tr., intransitively* = be of use, 202; *3d sing. pres. ind.* seruethe, 218; *p. pt.* serued, 47; = deserve, *p. pt.* serued, 186· seruethe, 194.

Seruyse, *sb.* = pay for service, 178.

Sethen. *See* Sythen

Sette, *v. tr.* = set, 73.

Seueneth, *adj.* = seventh, 42.

Seuenne, *numeral adj.* = seven, 61.

Sex, *numeral adj.* = six, 42, 144, 347. *See also* Six.

Sexte, *adj.* = sixth, 160; sixte, 168, 369.

Seyde. *See* Seye, *v. tr.*

Seye, *v. tr.* = say, 74; sey, 213; *3d sing. ind. pres.* seyth, 252; seythe, 162, 245; *3d pl.* seyn, 217; *3d sing. pf.* sayde, 25; seyde, 28, 50, 64, 67-8, 77, 82, 127, 131, 177, 193, 197, 208, 213, 346, 349.

Seyȝ *and* Seyȝe. *See* Se, *v. tr.*

Shafte, *sb.* 301.

Shake, *v. tr. 3d pl. pf. ind.* shoken, 356.

Shalle, *v. 1st sing. pres. ind.* 75, 78, 139, 212, 239, 261, 288, 299, 330; *2d sing.* shalt, 54, 80, 238,
260; *3d sing. pf.* sholde, 94, 129, 202, 224, 282; shulde, 37, 96, 103, 191; *3d pl.* sholde, 12.

Shanke, *sb., pl.* shankes, 326.

She, *pers. pron.* 10, 26, &c.

Shelde, *sb.* = shield, 281, 298, 331.

Shene, *adj.* = shining, beautiful, 8; sheene, 298.

Shoken. *See* Shake, *v. tr.*

Sholde = should. *See* Shalle.

Sholder, *sb.* 222, 334.

Shrykede, *3d sing. pf. ind.* of shryke (shriek), 81.

Shulde = should. *See* Shalle.

Shylde, *v. tr.* = shield, 298.

Shyuer, *v. tr.* = smash, splinter; *3d pl. pf. ind.* shyuereden, 315; *p. pt.* schyuered, 301.

Shyuereden. *See* Shyuer.

Six, *numeral adj.* 164, 193. *See* Sex.

Sixte, *adj.* = sixth, 369. *See also* Sexte.

Skape, *v. intr.* = escape, 127.

Sklawndered, *p. pt.* of sklawnder (slander); *v. tr.* = defame, accuse 234.

Skorne, *sb.* 264.

Skylfully, *adv.* 47.

Slepte, *3d sing. pf. ind.* of sleep, *v. intr.* 192.

Slongen, *3d pl. pf. ind.* of sling; *v. tr.* = to throw, 86; perhaps involving the idea of letting down by ropes; as we *sling* horses in a transport-ship, or as we suspend an arm in a *sling*.

Slyppe, *v. intr.* = slip, 52.

Small, *adj.* 307, 330.

Smerte, *sb.* = smart, 308.

Smertlye, *adv.* = smartly, sharply, 318. It is miswritten *smerlye* in the MS.

5

Smyte, *v. tr.*, 3d *sing. pf. ind.* smote, 146, 318; 3d *pl.* smoten, 327; 2d *sing. imper.* smyte, 311.

So, *adv.* 31, 70, 74, 103.

Sokour, *sb.* = succour, 111.

Somme, *adj.* = some, 111.

Sommene, *v. tr.* = summon, 187.

Sonde, *sb.* that which is sent, gift, 36.

Sone, *sb.* = son, 65, 78, 209, 347; sonne, 184, 211.

Soone, *adv.* 128, 208; sone, 105, 260-61.

Sorowefulle, *adj.* 91.

Sorwe, *sb.* = sorrow, 9; sorowe, 39, 78, 99, 359.

Sothe, *sb.* = truth, 18, 67, 131, 133, &c.

Sounde, *adj.* 43.

Sowke, *v. tr.* = suck, 115; *imp. pt.* sowkynge, 61.

Sowȝte. *See* Seche, *v.*

Speche, *sb.* 286.

Speke, *v. intr.* 249; 3d *sing. pres. ind.* 252.

Spere, *sb.* = spear, 263, 315.

Spin, *v. intr.* = rush quickly; 3d *sing. pres. indic.* spynnethe, 331. It is still used colloquially.

Spring, *v. intr.*, 3d *sing. pf. ind.* spronge, 331.

Spronge. *See* Spring.

Spynnethe. *See* Spin.

Staffe, *sb.* 220.

Stalworth, *adj.* = stalwart, strong, 326.

Stand, *v. intr.*, 3d *pl. pf. ind.* stoden, 147.

Stere, *v. intr.* = stir, move, 147.

Sterte, *v. intr.* = start; 3d *pl. pres. indic.* sterten, 356; 3d *pl. pf.* styrte, 326.

Steuenne, *sb.* = voice, 106, 149.

Stoden. *See* Stand.

Strawȝte. *See* Stretch.

Stretch, *v. intr.*, 3d *pl. pf. ind.* strawȝte, 220.

Strike, *v. tr.*, 3d *sing. pres. ind.* stryketh, 333; also *intransitively* = go; as we say, 'to strike across a field,' 229.

Stroke, *sb.* 333; *pl.* strokes, 298.

Stryketh. *See* Strike.

Styffe, *adj.* 241.

Styked, 3d *sing. pf. ind.* of stick *v. intr.* 241.

Stylle, *adj.* 147, 169.

Styrte. *See* Sterte.

Suche, *adj.* 202, 249, 264.

Sue, *v. tr.* = follow; 3d *sing pres. ind.* suwethe, 221; sueth 230.

Sum, *adj.* = some, 57.

Swanne, *sb.* 148, 198, 350, 356 358, 362.

Swerde, *sb.* = sword, 138, 146 304, 306-7, 327-8.

Swete, *adj.* 44.

Sworn, *p. pt.* of swear; *v. tr.* 236

Swyche, *adj.* = such, 49, 103 139.

Swyde *for* Swythe, *adv.* = quickly, 158.

Swyfte, *adv.* 113.

Swymmen, 3d *pl. pf. ind.* of swym (swim), 198, 350; 2d *sing pres.* swymmethe, 362.

Swyre, *sb.* = neck (O.E. *sweora*), 44, 126.

Syde, *sb.* 187.

Syken, *v. intr.* = to sigh; 3d *sing. pres. ind.* syketh, 66; 3d *sing. pf.* sykede, 25.

Syker, *adj.*, used *adverbially* = surely, 122.

Synne, *sb.* = sin, 250.

GLOSSARIAL INDEX.   35

Sythen (Sithen) = since, then, 13, 25, 53, 64, 199; sethen, 116.
Sytte, *v. intr.* 22, 293.
Syȝe. *See* Se, *v. tr.*
Syȝte, *sb.* = sight, 122, 188.

Taber, *sb.* = tabor, 226.
Take, *v. tr.* = betake, commend, 104; also in its usual sense, 262; *2d sing. imper.* 300; *3d sing. pres. ind.* taketh, 116; takethe, 63, 150; *1st sing. pf.* toke, 167; *2d sing.* tokest, 237; *3d sing.* toke, 159, 173, 229; *3d pl.* 355; token, 226; *p. pt.* taken, 234.
Tale, *sb.* 55.
Tawȝte, *p. pt.* of teche (teach), 312, 336.
Telle, *v. tr., 1st sing. pres. ind.* 162; *3d sing.* tellethe, 7, 270; *3d sing. pf.* tolde, 123, 347.
Tere, *sb.* = tear; *pl.* teres, 24.
Terme, *sb.* 140.
þanke, *sb.* = 194.
Thanke, *v. tr., 3d sing. pf. ind.* thanked, 339; þankede, 36.
þanne, *adv.* = then, at that time, 73, 210.
þat, *art.* = the, 159, 296, 322, 366; *rel. pron.* 3, 4; *dem. pron.* 18, 27, &c.; by þat, 248, 345 = by that time; *conj.* 16, 26, &c.
The, *art.* 7, 11, 17, &c.
The, *pers. pron. obj.* = thee, 18, 65, 73, 77–79, 134, 139-40, 169, 184, 230, 237, 261, 311, 312, 336.
The, *pers. pron.* = they, 220, 274.
þeder, *adv.* = thither, 265.
Thefe, *sb.* 141, 199, 351.
Thei, *pers. pron. See* They.
Thenke, *v.* = think, 30, 249 (Cp. Wm. 4908); Germ. *denken;* *2d sing. pf. ind.* thowȝte, 40, 207, 250, 264.
þenne, *conj.* = than, 125; *adv.* = when, 143; = at that time, 24,
41, 63, 67, &c.; ere thenne, 330 = before the time when; by thenne, 143 = by that time; = thence, 248.
þerby, *adv.* = near there, 265.
þere, *adv.* 13, 31, 87; = where, 76, 96, 121, 142, 362.
Therfore, *adv.* = on that account, 136.
þerin, *adv.* 52, 247.
þerof, *adv.* 115.
þerupon, *adv.* 282.
þese, *dem. pron. pl.* 93, 179, &c.
þey, *pers. pron. pl.* 12, 19, &c.; thei, 326. *See also* The.
This, *dem. pron.* 5, 92; er þis, 70 = before now.
Thoo, *adv.* = then, at that time, 339.
þorow, *prep.* = through, 95, 170.
þou, *pers. pron.* 50—54, &c.; thow, 80, 251.
þowghe, *conj.* = though, 100.
Thowȝte. *See* Thenke.
Thrydde, *adj.* = third, 367.
þus, *adv.* 89, 118.
þy, *poss. pron.* 65, 73.
Thykke, *adj.* = thick (closely covered), 294.
Thylle, *conj.* = till, 96.
Thynge, *sb.* 30, 202.
To, *prep.* 16, 17, &c.
Togedere, *adv.* = together, 20, 314; togedur, 327.
Toke } *See* Take.
Token }
Topseyle, *adv.* = headlong, 320. *See* Note.
Towarde, *prep.* 33, 93, 109, 341.
Towre, *sb.* 280.
Trewe, *adj.* = true, 48, 69.
Trist, *v. tr.* = trust; *3d sing. pf. ind.* triste, 49; truste, 285.

Trowthe, *sb.* = truth, 175.
Trumpe, *sb.* = trumpet, 226.
Truss, *v. tr.* to remove (Cotgrave, trousser, to trusse, tuck, packe, bind, or gird in, pluck, or twitch up); 3*d sing. pres. ind.* trussethe, 327.
Truste, *v. tr.* 3*d sing. pf. ind.* 285.
Tryfulle, *v. intr.* = trifle, 48.
Tumbledde, 3*d pl. pf. ind.* of tumble; *v. intr.* 320.
Turne, *sb.* in a good sense (as we say, 'to do one a good turn'), 139; in a bad sense, trick, wile, 257.
Turne, *v. tr.*, 3*d sing. pres. ind.* turneth, 262; 3*d sing. pf.* turned, 24, 341; *intr.* 3*d pres. ind.* 104, 150; 3*d pl.* turnen, 355, 357; 3*d sing. pf.* turnede, 123; 1*st pl. imper.* turne, 93.
Twelfe, *numeral adj.* 243.
Tweyne, *numeral adj.* = two, twain, 29, 84.
Two, *numeral adj.* 23, 27, &c.; in two, 334.
Twynleng, *sb.* = a little twin, 27.
Tydynge, *sb.* 59; *pl.* tydynges, 58.
Tylle, *conj.* 310.
Tymber, *sb.* 317.
Tyme, *sb.* = time, 37, 55, 243.
Tyraunte, *sb.* = wicked, or evil man, 84. In Allit. the people of Sodom are called *tyrants*, B. 943.
Tyte, *adj.* = quick, 139. It is used here *adverbially.*
Tytlye, *adv.* = quickly, 84.

Unbounden, *p. pt.* of unbind; *v. tr.* 345.
Unbrente, *adj.* = unburnt, 185.
Under, *adv.* 21.
Undo = undone, *p. pt.* of undone, *v. tr.* = undo, 105.
Unsemelye, *adj.* 30.

Unto, *prep.* 90.
Unwerkethe, *adj.* = unworked, 175.
Up, *prep.* 64, 81, 97, &c.
Upon, *prep.* 19, 213, 222, 236, 281; = with, 361.

Valwe, *sb.* = value, 329.

Wakynge, *imp. pt.* of wake; *v. intr.* 207.
Walle, *sb.* 19, 349.
Ware, *adj.* 122.
Warne, *v. tr.* 190.
Was, 3*d sing. pf. ind.* of be, 5, 6, &c.
Water, *sb.* 355, 362 = a piece of water, 51, 96.
We, *pers. pron. pl.* 3, 92, 302.
Wedde, *v. tr.* = bet, pledge, 27; *p. pt.* wedded = married, 69.
Wede, *sb.* = dress, clothing, 119; *pl.* wedes.
Wele, *adv.* = well, 2, 54, 67, 140, 309, 352; welle, 251.
Well, *v. intr.* = to bubble, pour forth copiously (O.E. *welan* = to boil); 3*d sing. pf. indic.* wellede, 166.
Welle, *adv.* 251.
Wende, *v. intr.* = go, 206; 3*d sing. pres. indic.* wendes, 155, 178; wendethe, 161; wendeth, 190 (*see* Note); 3*d pl. pres. indic.* wenden, 302, 364; 2*d sing imper.* wende, 137.
Wene, *v. intr.* = ween, thinke (O.E. *wenan*); 1*st sing pres. ind.* wene, 69; 3*d sing. pf. indic.* wente, 67.
Wenten, 3*d pl. pf. ind.*, serving as past tense of go; *v. intr.* 33; wente, 19; 3*d sing.* (*reflexively* used) 75.
Were, 3*d pl. pf. ind.* of be, 41, 58, 142; 3*d sing. pf. subj.* 30, 67,

156; 3*d pl.* 31; used for wast, 2*d sing. pf. ind.* 237 ; 3*d pl. pf. ind.* weren, 121.

Weren, *v. tr.* = defend (O.E. *werian;* Germ. *wehren*) ; 3*d sing. pres. ind.* wereth, 2.

Werke, *sb.* = work, 2, 170, 330 (Germ. *werke*).

Werke, *v. tr.* = work, 78, 182 (O. Germ. *werken*).

Werue, *v. tr.* = deny, refuse (O.E. *wyrnan*), 56, 72.

Wesselle, *sb.* = vessel ; or else silver plate. Fr. *vaisselle,* 156.

Wex, *v. intr.* = to wax, to grow ; 3*d sing. pres. indic.* wexeth, 158 ; *pf.* wexedde, 166.

Wey, *sb.* = way, 220.

Wey3te, *sb.* = weight, 155.

What, *rel. pron.* 56 ; *interrog.* 74.

Whelpe, *sb.* 61 ; welpe, 63.

Whenne, *adv.* = when, 1, 12, &c.

Where, *adv.* 12 ; *interrog.* 82.

Whyle, *adv.* 273 ; whyles, 145 ; whylle, 117 ; *sb.* 286.

Whyte, *adj.* 281.

With, *prep.* 2, 28, &c. ; withe, 14, 23, &c.; wyth, 99.

Witty, *adj.* = cheerful (?), 35.

Wo, *sb.* 343.

Wolle, *v.* ; 1*st sing. pres. ind.* 244; 3*d sing.* 252; 2*d sing.* wolt, 72 ; 3*d sing. pf. ind.* wolde, 30, 41, 56, 117, 164, 276. *See* Wylle.

Womman, *sb.* = woman, 22, 26, 38; *pl.* wymmen, 29.

Wondrethe, 3*d sing. pres. ind.* of wonder; *v. intr.* 184.

Wonnen. *See* Wynne, *v. tr.*

Woode, *sb.* 113 ; wode, 119, 143, 215.

Worde, *sb.* 193, 207, 349 ; *pl.* worthes, 32.

Worlde, *sb.* 112, 180, 184.

Worse, *adj.* 244.

Worthes. *See* Word.

Wrake, *sb.* = punishment, 72. It is coupled with wrech = vengeance, in Gen. 552.

Wrecche, *sb.* = wretch, 71.

Wrecched, *adj.* = wretched, 77.

Wronge, *sb.* 245 ; *adj.* used *adverbially* = wrongly, 170, 197, 349.

Wrow3te = wrought, 3*d sing. pf. ind.* of work, 119.

Wryten, *p. pt.* of wryte ; *v. tr.* 282.

Wyfe, *sb.* = wife, 69, 162, 169, 196.

Wylde, *adj.* 214.

Wyle, *sb.* = wile, 182.

Wylle, *sb.* = will, 1, 79, 181, &c.

Wylle, *v.* ; 1*st sing. pres. ind.* 128, 261; 2*d sing.* 290; 2*d sing.* wylt, 260. *See* Wolle.

Wynne, *v. tr.* = win; *p. pt.* wonnen, 170 ; 3*d sing. pres. ind.* wynnethe = getteth, taketh, 337 ; thus miners speak of winning or getting out ores, or coals.

Wyse, *sb.* = wise, manner, 156.

Wyste. *See* Wytte.

Wyte, *v. tr.* = blame, 136.

Wytte, *v. tr.* = know ; 2*d sing. imper.* 195 ; 2*d sing. pf. ind.* wysste, 35 ; 3*d pl. pf.* wyste, 274 ; 2*d sing. pf. subj.* 186.

Yen, *sb.* = eyen, eyne *or* eyes, 135, 323, 332.

Yf, *conj.* = if, 54.

Yle, *sb.* = isle, 5.

Yren, *sb.* = iron, 290.

3afe, 3*d pl. pf. ind.* of give, 271.

3ate, *sb.* = gate, 22.

3e = yea, 212, 302.

3elde, *v. tr.* = yield, 335, 336. *See* Note.

ʒere, *sb.* = year, 89, 243.

ʒonder, *adj.* (preceded by an *article*) = yonder, 26; ʒondur, 232; ʒondere, 233; *adv.* 198, 350.

ʒonge, *adj.* = young, 81, 242, 251, 345.

ʒosken, *v. intr.* = to hiccough, t(sob; 3*d pl. pf. ind.* ʒoskened, 108.

ʒou, *pers. pron. obj.* = you, 100.

ʒyf, *conj.* = if, 235.

ʒyfte, *sb.* = gift, 271.

ʒys = yes, 309

The manufacturer's authorised representative in the EU for product safety is Oxford University Press España S.A. of El Parque Empresarial San Fernando de Henares, Avenida de Castilla, 2 - 28830 Madrid (www.oup.es/en or product.safety@oup.com). OUP España S.A. also acts as importer into Spain of products made by the manufacturer.
Printed and bound by CPI Group (UK) Ltd, Croydon, CR0 4YY

20/03/2026

02075329-0005